THE
O... MAINE

Joël Pomerleau

ULYSSES
TRAVEL PUBLICATIONS
Travel better... enjoy more

Series Director Claude Morneau	*English Translation* Tracy Kendrick Sarah Kresh	*Artistic Director* Patrick Farei Atoll Direction
Project Supervisor Pascale Couture	*Cartography* André Duchesne	*Collaboration* Virginie Bonneau
Research and *Composition* Joël Pomerleau	*Assistant* Steve Rioux	*Illustrations* Marie-Annik Viatour
English Editor Jennifer McMorran	*Layout* Christian Roy	*Photography* *Cover* Camerique - Perkins Cove

Special thanks to: Carol Arena; Nancy Marshall (Maine Visitor's Bureau); Brigitte Thériault; Isabelle Lalonde and the Hors Champs team. Ulysses Travel Publications thank SODEC (Québec government) and the Canadian Heritage Minister for their financial support.

Distributors

AUSTRALIA:
Little Hills Press
11/37-43 Alexander St.
Crows Nest NSW 2065
☎ (612) 437-6995
Fax: (612) 438-5762

BELGIUM AND LUXEMBOURG:
Vander
Vrijwilligerlaan 321
B-1150 Brussel
☎ (02) 762 98 04
Fax: (02) 762 06 62

CANADA:
Ulysses Books & Maps
4176 Saint-Denis
Montréal, Québec
H2W 2M5
☎ (514) 843-9882,
ext.2232
Fax: 514-843-9448
http://www.ulysse.ca

GERMANY AND AUSTRIA:
Brettschneider
Fernreisebedarf
Feldfirchner Strasse 2
D-85551 Heimstetten
München
☎ 89-99 02 03 30
Fax: 89-99 02 03 31

GREAT BRITAIN AND IRELAND:
World Leisure Marketing
9 Downing Road
West Meadows, Derby
UK DE21 6HA
☎ 1 332 34 33 32
Fax: 1 332 34 04 64

ITALY:
Edizioni del Riccio
Via di Soffiano 164 A
50143 Firenze
☎ (055) 71 33 33
Fax: (055) 71 63 50

NETHERLANDS:
Nilsson & Lamm
Pampuslaan 212-214
1380 AD Weesp (NL)
☎ 0294-465044
Fax: 0294-415054

SCANDINAVIA:
Scanvik
Esplanaden 8B
1263 Copenhagen K
DK
☎ (45) 33.12.77.66
Fax: (45) 33.91.28.82

SPAIN:
Altaïr
Balmes 69
E-08007 Barcelona
☎ 454 29 66
Fax: 451 25 59

SWITZERLAND:
OLF
P.O. Box 1061
CH-1701 Fribourg
☎ (026) 467.51.11
Fax: (026) 467.54.66

U.S.A.:
The Globe Pequot Press
6 Business Park Road
P.O. Box 833
Old Saybrook, CT 06475
☎ 1-800-243-0495
Fax: 1-800-820-2329

Other countries, contact Ulysses Books & Maps (Montréal), Fax: (514) 843-9448
Canadian Cataloguing in Press see p 6

TABLE OF CONTENTS

"What other State compares with Maine
In glorious coasts, where ocean tides
Have for long ages beat in vain
To storm the coves where safety hides;
Where pillared cliffs like sentries stand
To guard the entries to the land,
From Kittery to Calais!"

Nathan Haskell Dole (1852-1935)
The State of Maine

LIST OF MAPS

Canadian Cataloguing in Publication Data
Joël Pomerleau, 1974-
　　　Beaches of Maine
　　　(Ulysses Travel Guides)
　　　Includes index.
　　　Translation of: Plages du Maine
　　　ISBN 2-89464-066-8
1. Maine - Guidebooks.　I. Title.　II. Series.
F17.3.P6513 1997　　917.4104'43　　C97-940020-1

TABLE OF SYMBOLS

☎	Telephone number
⊨	Fax number
≡	Air conditioning
⊗	Ceiling fan
≈	Pool
ℜ	Restaurant
⊛	Whirlpool
ℝ	Refrigerator
K	Kitchenette
△	Sauna
⊘	Exercise room
tv	Colour television
pb	Private bathroom
sb	Shared bathroom
ps	Private shower
½b	half-board (lodging + 2 meals)
bkfst	Breakfast

ATTRACTION CLASSIFICATION

★	Interesting
★★	Worth a visit
★★★	Not to be missed

HOTEL CLASSIFICATION

Unless otherwise indicated, the prices in the guide
are for one room in the high season,
double occupancy, not including taxes.

RESTAURANT CLASSIFICATION

$	$8 or less
$$	$8 to $16
$$$	$16 to $24
$$$$	$24 or more

Unless otherwise indicated, the prices in the guide are for a
meal for one person, including taxes, but not drinks and tip.

All prices in this guide are in American dollars.

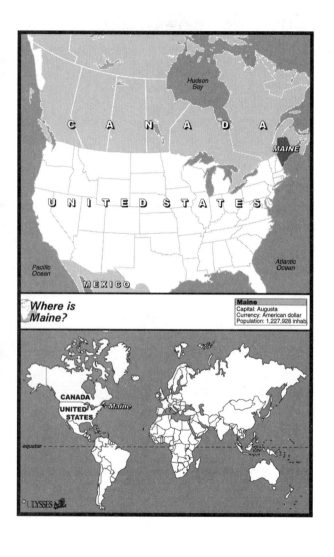

Where is Maine?

Maine
Capital: Augusta
Currency: American dollar
Population: 1,227,928 inhab.

PORTRAIT

The coast of Maine is one of the most popular destinations in the United States, yet also one of the most poorly known. It is a sort of northern Riviera for Canadians and Americans in search of a little surf and sand. And that about sums up how most people think of the coast of Maine: a stretch of beaches for the urbanites of the northeastern part of the continent. But how does one describe the stunning beauty of the region's scenery, the sound of the waves pounding the shore at high tide or the refreshing breeze of an autumn morning? What words could possibly do justice to those magnificent powdery beaches, a subtle, luminous line between the ocean and the sky?

The goal of this guide is to acquaint you with the southern coast of Maine, with the forgotten little seaside hamlets and with the pristine parks at the end of small coastal roads. Those who take the time to explore the coast of Maine will discover all sorts of treasures cradled by the waves and infused with the salty sea air.

GEOGRAPHY

The state of Maine is bounded by the Canadian provinces of Québec to the northwest and New Brunswick to the northeast, by the state of New Hampshire to the southwest and by the Atlantic Ocean to the southeast. It covers an area of 86,156 square kilometres. Augusta is the state capital, though Portland is the largest city. Lewiston and Bangor are the second and third biggest cities respectively.

There are four distinct geographical regions in Maine: the coastal lowlands, the piedmont, the mountains and the uplands. This state, like the greater part of both Canada and the rest of the northern United States, was shaped by a glacier that covered the region over one million years ago. At its peak, this glacier was nearly 1.5 kilometres thick. It started to recede nearly 18,000 years later, leaving behind a territory strewn with some 6,000 lakes and ponds, and 51,500 kilometres of rivers, with piles of sand or stone here and there. The coastal lowlands are a strip of land barely 25 kilometres wide and 5,565 kilometres long.

The Atlantic coast of Maine, with its hundreds of kilometres of powdery beaches, is no myth. Though the state's forests are undeniably beautiful, people come here for the sand and surf. Lit up by its famous lighthouses and punctuated with little fishing bays, it continues to captivate visitors.

The origin of the word "Maine" remains vague. Some people claim that it comes from the sailors' term for the continent, the mainland, while others believe that French colonists named the region after the French province of the same name.

FLORA

As forests cover 80% of Maine, this resource naturally plays a crucial role in the local economy. The woods are mainly comprised of coniferous trees such as tamarack, white spruce, fir, hemlock and white pine. A few hardwood species can also be found in the region (beech, birch, red maple, sugar maple, white oak, etc).

FAUNA

Maine is still home to a large herd of white-tailed deer, although hunters kill nearly 30,000 each year. Moose, Canada lynx, black bears, beavers, muskrats, raccoons, skunks, red foxes, hares and various species of rodents also live here. The lakes and rivers are teeming with trout and salmon, while the Atlantic coast is inhabited by seals, whales and a whole colony of shellfish including, notably, the famous Maine lobster.

A BRIEF HISTORY

The first inhabitants of the American continent migrated from Asia. Most historians agree that the Amerindian peoples are descendants of Mongolians who crossed the Bering Strait over 25,000 year ago, when the strait was a strip of land linking Asia and America. Numerous archaeological excavations carried out in Maine have revealed evidence of human activity dating from the Palaeolithic age. These "Red Paint People", thus named because of the red ochre found in their tombs, apparently died out long before the Abenaki arrived.

The Abenaki, a branch of the Algonquin nation, were divided up into about a dozen tribes with a total of about 35,000 people. They inhabited the regions now known as Maine, New Hampshire and Vermont, as well as part of Canada. The Abenaki spent the winter in the forest and the summer on the coast, where they fished for shellfish. The Abenaki were on friendly terms with the first British colonists. However, the early 17th century was a tragic period for several native nations. A large number of Abenakis were wiped out by a war with the neighbouring nation, the Tarrantines, in 1614 and 1615, and a smallpox epidemic in 1617. Furthermore, France developed very close ties with the natives, which made subsequent interaction between the Abenaki and the British colonists somewhat stormy.

The Vikings were the first Europeans to set foot on American soil (c. 1000). On his way to convert the people of Greenland to Christianity, Leif Ericsson was caught out by adverse winds and ended up in a region where vines and wheat were growing wild. He named the territory "Vinland". His curiosity piqued by Ericsson's accounts, Throfin Karlsefni set sail for the new country. As promised, he found a rich, fertile land. The Vikings' initial interaction with the natives involved bartering for fur and cloth. However, at the first sign of conflict, the bewildered Europeans took off. Although there are many accounts of these

Viking adventures, it is impossible to determine the exact location of Vinland. As there is no mention of Vikings in the native oral tradition and no one can identify the *shrellings* (dwarves) alluded to in the Viking narratives, some historians doubt that the Vikings ever made it farther than Nova Scotia.

Everyone agrees, however, that Giovanni de Verrazano came here in 1524. From then on, English and French fishermen started sailing the Gulf of Maine. A little later, some of them began spending the winter on the shore so that they could fish longer. The first attempts at establishing a permanent village date back to 1604 for the French and 1607 for the English; both failed. Numerous other less formal attempts at colonization were equally unsuccessful until finally, in 1630, a group managed to settle on the islands of Monhegan and Damariscove.

Sir Ferdinando Gorges, then president of the Council of New England, was the first to be granted the territory now known as Maine. He and Captain John Mason divided up the land between the Merrimack and Kennebeck Rivers at the Piscataqua River. Gorges founded the Province of Mayne and spent the rest of his life vainly trying to govern the territory by dividing it up according to a feudal system. Shortly after his death in 1647, the government of the Massachusetts Bay Colony annexed Maine upon the consent of the region's small coastal villages. Massachusetts then purchased the title to Maine from Gorges's heirs in 1677, and the annexation was made official in the Massachusetts provincial charter in 1691.

In those days, Maine was sparsely inhabited—a region yet to be conquered, a region torn apart by the incessant wars between the British and the French and native coalition. For its first century of colonization, Maine had an economy based solely on fishing, trading and the exploitation of forest resources. Toward the 1730s, Great Britain's supply centre for white pine was moved from Portsmouth, New Hampshire, to Falmouth (now Portland), Maine. Around the same time, the region's first shipyard opened in Falmouth, and the first inland villages were founded.

British hegemony in New England began to be threatened in the 1770s. In Maine particularly, there was a surge in revolutionary sentiment when London decided to hand Louisbourg, an important French fortress captured by a Yankee expedition in 1745, back over to France. Furthermore, numerous conflicts, sometimes violent, had been erupting between woodsmen and British authorities trying to enforce royal timber laws. The combination of these two situations prompted fierce opposition to the Crown. In June 1775, the townspeople of Macchias captured the British frigate *Margaretta* during the first naval conflict of the American Revolution. In response to this affront, a British naval squadron set fire to the port of Falmouth in October 1775, destroying nearly three quarters of the town. This reprisal only strengthened the 13 colonies' desire for independence.

In the fall of 1775, Colonel Benedict Arnold led an expedition up the Kennebec River to Québec. At the same time, another group sailed up Lake Champlain and the St. Lawrence River toward Montréal. The goal of these two simultaneous expeditions was to drive the English out of Québec and draw the French and the natives into the war. Their efforts failed, and they abandoned the siege in the summer of 1776. The second major event that took place in Maine during the Revolutionary War was another notorious American failure. During the summer of 1779, a naval battalion led by Captain Richard Saltonstall tried to dislodge the English forces from Castine, on the east coast of Penobscot Bay. The British held out, and in August another English squadron arrived on the scene and drove off the Americans.

Maine's desire to become an independent state emerged in 1785, but it wasn't until the War of 1812 that this became a goal shared by the general populace. Finally, after several attempts, William King succeeded in rallying a vast majority to vote for independence in an 1819 referendum. Maine's admission into the Union was complicated by southern pressure to maintain a balance between slave states and free states. It was finally agreed that there should be an equal number of southern and northern states. Maine, a free state, was thus admitted to the Union concurrently with Missouri, a slave state, in 1820, at which time William King became the first governor of the state of Maine.

Maine's first years of statehood were very prosperous. The region continued to enjoy an economic boom that had begun shortly after the American Revolution. Massive immigration from Massachusetts and New Hampshire, the revival of the shipbuilding industry after the 1807 embargo, the staggering growth of the timber industry and the development of agriculture all helped ensure the state a future full of promise.

During the 1830s, a serious conflict nearly broke out over the issue of the Maine-New Brunswick border, but was fortunately averted by the signing of the Webster-Ashburton Treaty in 1842. Around the same time, Portland native Neil Dow managed to get a prohibition law—the first of its kind in a western country—ratified in Maine. The anti-slavery cause also found sympathizers in Maine. It was in this liberationist spirit that Harriet Beecher Stowe, born in the town of Brunswick, wrote *Uncle Tom's Cabin* in 1851. Abraham Lincoln himself referred to Stowe as the "little lady who started a big war".

The opening of textile and shoe factories (1830-1860) marked the start of Maine's industrialization. After the Civil War, the paper industry underwent a major revolution, and Maine became one of the biggest pulp and paper producers in North America. This explains why a few giant companies now own half the woodlands in Maine. This period coincided with a massive influx of French-Canadian immigrants into New England. Between 1860 and 1930, nearly 750,000 Quebecers left Canada to come try their luck in American factories.

This century has been marked by the rapid development of the tourist industry. Wealthy vacationers had already discovered Bar Harbor and Boothbay by the end of the 19th century, but it wasn't until the 1920s that Maine started becoming a popular destination among the general public. The tourist industry is still growing today. Finally, in recent years the political scene has been marked by disputes between environmentalists and proponents of economic development.

POLITICS

The constitution of the state of Maine, based on that of Massachusetts, was adopted in 1819.

The bicameral legislature, made up of a senate with 31 to 35 members (in proportion to the number of districts) and a house of representatives with 151 members, convenes every two years to choose the secretary of state, the attorney general and the state treasurer. All legislators are elected for two-year terms.

The governor, whose term lasts four years, is the only representative elected by statewide ballot; all citizens 18 and over are eligible to vote. The office can be held for a maximum of two consecutive terms.

ECONOMY

With its vast expanses of woodlands, Maine naturally produces pulp and paper—more than any other state in the country, for that matter. The state is also home to numerous food-processing, textile and lumber companies, and there are large shipyards in the towns of Bath and Kittery. Agriculture plays an important role in the local economy as well, with potato and poultry farming clearly in the lead. Other activities include stockbreeding, dairy farming and apple-growing.

Thanks to Maine's long Atlantic shoreline, fishing is the third most important sector of the state economy. Lobster, which makes up only 10% of the total catch, accounts for nearly half the industry's revenue. A few non-metallic ores, including quartz, graphite, asbestos, topaz and granite, which has always been an important product, given its frequent use throughout the United States, are found in certain parts of the state, though the mining industry employs a very small number of people. Finally, tourism is obviously of central importance to the local economy. Thanks to the state's lovely beaches, about 6% of the population works in the industry.

POPULATION

The population of Maine consists primarily of descendants of British, Scottish and Irish colonists. The values, language and culture of rural New England are still very much alive here—more so than in most other parts of the United States. The descendants of French-speaking Quebecers are the most prominent minority by far, accounting for 20% of the total population. A very small percentage of the population (less than 1%) is black. Nearly 5,000 natives also live in Maine.

The majority of the population is Protestant (Baptist, Congregationalist, Methodist, Episcopalian and Universalist), and nearly 30% is Roman Catholic. The number of Jews and orthodox Christians remains limited.

ARTS

Visual Arts

As far as the visual arts are concerned, Maine certainly can't claim the oldest tradition in the United States. As the state was colonized fairly late, few artists settled here early on. At first, the members of the upper class called upon renowned painters from Boston and New York to immortalize their family according to British custom. At the same time, popular artists such as Orison Wood, Rufus Porter, John Brewster, Jonathan Fisher and Suzan Pains were starting to emerge in the region. These artists went to the countryside to immortalize the region on canvas; travelling inland was an adventure in itself back in those days, so they deserve that much more credit.

The 19th century saw the emergence of a few renowned sculptors, notably Paul Akers and Edward Augustus Bracket. A number of painters also came here to draw inspiration from the beauty of the Atlantic coast, while a few local artists established a name for themselves in the region. The industrialization that marked the end of the 19th century had a stifling effect on the regional art scene, however. Standardized methods of mass production led to the elimination of many crafts that reflected local culture. On the other hand, this new technology forced artists to become specialized, and it was thus that a number of painters gained public recognition. One notable example was Anna Elizabeth Hardy, who won renown for her still lifes.

At the beginning of the 20th century, painters influenced by the impressionist movement in France began arriving in the region. One of the most noteworthy of these was Childe Hasam, who spent several summers on the islands off Kittery studying shape, light and colour. Many other impressionists also came to the coast of Maine to paint. The portraiture tradition continued, but was now carried on by local artists, who immortalized the daily life of Maine residents. The emergence of European splinter movements, such as cubism and expressionism, prompted many American artists to set off for France to study with the masters. Some of these returned to the coast of Maine, but did not stay here for long.

Since the mid-20th century, all different manner of visual arts have developed in Maine. Though cubism and abstraction were fashionable in the 1930s and 1940s, many artists remained loyal to the region's pictorial traditions. Today, like everywhere else, Maine is home to painters, sculptors and other artists of all sorts, thus earning itself a growing place in American art history.

Literature

Maine's literary and cultural scene has been profoundly influenced by three famous figures: Harriet Beecher Stowe, Henry Wadsworth Longfellow and Kenneth Roberts. Abraham Lincoln dubbed Stowe "the little lady who started a big war". A law instituted in 1850, which made it compulsory to denounce escaped slaves, inspired her to write **Uncle Tom's Cabin**, published in serial form in *The National Era* in 1851. The series provoked a great deal of controversy in the period leading up to the Civil War. It was translated into 32 languages and adapted for the stage. Harriet Beecher Stowe's achievement lies mainly in the debate she unleashed. Over time, however, African Americans have come to view *Uncle Tom's Cabin* as a symbol of colonialist paternalism.

An undeniably fascinating man, Kenneth Roberts penned the novels *Arundel*, *Rabble in Arms*, *Northwest Passage* and *Oliver Wiswell*. Born in Kennebunk, he wrote rich, essentially popular fiction inspired by local history. It was thanks to a writer friend, Booth Tarkinton, that Roberts, originally a journalist, turned to novels. As Tarkinton was nearly blind, Roberts would read aloud to him, and the two friends would then put the finishing touches on the characters and story together. *Arundel* and the three subsequent novels make up the *Chronicles of Arundel*, an historical series in which Roberts retraces his ancestors' past, from their arrival in North America to the American Revolution. It was in honour of this author that the town of North Kennebunk was renamed Arundel.

In addition to being a talented writer, Roberts was also quite a character. He detested all the noises of modern life, and his house at Kennebunk Beach did not protect him adequately from his fans. Among the things he couldn't stand were lawnmowers, golfers, children's shouts, the telephone and airplanes (he supposedly went outside once to shoot at an airplane with his hunting gun). Fortunately, the commercial success of his last books enabled him to build himself a more cloistered retreat. He was the first person responsible for the ban on billboards along the state highways. It is to wonder what he would think of Maine's self-assigned nickname, "Vacationland"!

Henry Wadsworth Longfellow, another key figure in the history of American literature, was born in Portland. He studied foreign languages at Bowdoin College, then set off to tour Europe. Upon his return, he helped popularize European culture in North America, publishing a series of travel sketches entitled *Outre-Mer: A Pilgrimage beyond the Sea* (1835). Longfellow became the first American poet to earn his living writing poetry; he was also one of his country's most "official" authors. His work is characterized by didacticism and the presence of American heros.

PRACTICAL INFORMATION

I nformation in this section will help visitors from English-speaking countries better plan their trip to the beaches of Maine.

ENTRANCE FORMALITIES

Travellers from Canada, the majority of western European countries, Australia and New Zealand do not need visas to enter the United States. A valid passport is sufficient for stays of up to three months. A return ticket and proof of sufficient funds to cover your stay may be required. For stays of more than three months, all travellers, except Canadians and citizens of the British Commonwealth, must obtain a visa ($120 US) from the American embassy in their country.

Caution: as medical expenses can be very high in the United States, travel health insurance is highly recommended. For more information, see the section entitled "Health" (p 29).

CUSTOMS

Foreigners may enter the United States with 200 cigarettes (or 100 cigars) and duty-free purchases not exceeding $400 US, including personal gifts and 1 litre of alcohol (you must be 21 years of age to drink alcohol). There is no limit on the amount of cash you are carrying, though you must fill out a special form if you are carrying the equivalent of more than $10,000 US. Prescription medication must be placed in containers clearly marked to that effect (you may have to produce a prescription or a written statement from your doctor to customs officials). Meat and its by-products, all kinds of food, grains, plants, fruits and narcotics can not be brought into the United States.

For more ample information, contact:

United States Customs Service 1301 Constitution Avenue Northwest, Washington, DC 20229, ☎ (202) 566-8195

EMBASSIES AND CONSULATES

United States Embassies and Consulates Abroad

Australia United States Embassy, Moonah Place, Canberra, ACT 2600, ☎ 270-5000

Belgium United States Embassy, 27 Boulevard du Régent, B-100 Brussels, ☎ (2) 513-3830, ≈ (2) 511-2725

Canada: United States Embassy, 2 Wellington Street, Ottawa, Ontario, K1P 5T1, ☎ (613) 238-5335, ≈ (613) 238-5720.

United States Consulate, Place Félix-Martin, 1155 Rue Saint-Alexandre, Montréal, Québec, H2Z 1Z2, ☎ (514) 398-9695, ≈ (514) 398-9748.

United States Consulate, 360 University Avenue, Toronto, Ontario, M5G 1S4, ☎ (416) 595-1700, ≈ (416) 595-0051.

United States Consulate, 1095 West Pender, Vancouver, British Columbia, V6E 2M6, ☎ (604) 685-4311.

Germany: United States Embassy, Deichmans Aue 29, 53170 Bonn, ☎ 228-3391.

Great Britain: United States Embassy, 24 Grosvenor Square, London W1A 1AE, ☎ 171-499-9000.

Ireland: United States Embassy, 42 Elgin Road, Ballsbridge, Dublin, ☎ 668-7122.

Italy: United States Embassy, Via Veneto 121, 00187 Roma, ☎ (06) 46741.

Netherlands: United States Embassy, Lange Voorhout 102, Den Haag, ☎ (70) 310-9209.

New Zealand: United States Embassy, 29 Fitzherbert Terrace, Thorndon, Wellington, ☎ 472-2068.

Spain: United States Embassy, C. Serrano 75, Madrid, 28006, ☎ 587-2200.

Switzerland: United States Embassy, 93 Jubilam Strasse, 3000 Berne, ☎ 31-43-70-11.

Foreign Consulates in Boston or New York City

Australia: Consulate, 630 5th Avenue, New York, NY 10111, ☎ (212) 408-8400.

Belgium: Consulate, 300 Commonwealth Ave., Boston, MA 02116, ☎ (617) 266-1680, ⇆ (617) 437-1090.

Canada: Consulate, 3 Copeley Place, suite 400, Boston, Ma 02116, ☎ (617) 262-3760, ⇆ (617) 262-3415.

Great Britain: Consulate, 25th Floor Federal Reserve Place, 600 Atlantic Avenue, Boston, MA 02210, ☎ (617) 248-9555, ⇆ (617) 248-9578.

Italy: Consulate, 690 Park Avenue, New York, NY 10021, ☎ (212) 737-9100, ≈ (212) 249-4945.

Netherlands: Consulate, 6 Saint-James Ave., 3rd floor, Boston, MA 02116, ☎ (617) 542-8452, ≈ (617) 542-3304.

New Zealand: Consulate, 37 Observatory Circle NW, Washington, DC 20008, ☎ (202) 328-4000.

Spain: Consulate, 545 Boylston, suite 803, Boston, MA 02116, ☎ (617) 536-2506, ≈ (617) 536-8512.

Switzerland: Consulate, 665 5th Avenue, New York, NY 10021, ☎ (212) 758-2560, ≈ (212) 207-8024.

 ## TOURIST INFORMATION

Information is available directly from the Maine tourist office or from the various local chambers of commerce.

Maine Publicity Bureau P.O. Box 2300, Hallowell, ME 04347, ☎ (207) 623-0363, or toll-free 1-800-533-9595 (in North America), ≈ (207) 623-0388.

Kittery and Eliot Chamber of Commerce 191 State Road, Kittery, ME 03904, ☎ 439-7545.

York Chamber of Commerce P.O. Box 417, York, ME 03909, ☎ 363-4422.

Ogunquit Chamber of Commerce P.O. Box 2289, Ogunquit, ME 03907, ☎ 646-2939 or 646-5139.

Wells Chamber of Commerce P.O. Box 356, Wells, ME 04090, ☎ 646-2451.

Kennebunk-Kennebunkport Chamber of Commerce 173 Port Road, P.O. Box 740, Kennebunk, ME 04043, ☎ 967-0857.

Old Orchard Chamber of Commerce P.O. Box 600, Old Orchard Beach, ME 04064, ☎ 934-2500.

The Convention and Visitors Bureau of Greater Portland
305 Commercial Street, Portland, ME 04101, ☎ 772-5800.

GETTING THERE

By Plane

International flights serve New York City and Boston. Once there, connecting shuttle flights are available to Portland.

Airports

Portland International Jetport is the largest airport on the Maine coast. It is served by US Air, Continental Airlines, Delta Airlines and United Airlines. Each of these companies offers two to three flights per day to Portland. They also offer shuttle flights between Portland and New York and Boston. The airport is located 15 minutes from downtown. Taxis, limousines and city buses provide transportation into downtown. For information call ☎ (207) 774-7301.

Boston's **Logan International Airport** is the only international airport in New England and therefore the closest one to the Maine coast. It is located close to downtown Boston. This modern airport is served by most major airlines. You have several options to reach downtown Boston: taxi, limousine, bus and subway. For the latter, you must take the **Massport Shuttle Bus**, which will leave at the closest subway station free of charge. A subway trip costs $0.85.

By Car

Interstate 95 follows the Maine coast from the New Hampshire border north to Brunswick where it heads inland and continues north. Visitors arriving from points north or west will most likely enter the state of Maine on **Route 302** or **Route 26** and then **Route 202**.

FINDING YOUR WAY AROUND

Table of Distances

Boston					
151	Kennebunk				
521	365	Montréal			
110	20	345	Ogunquit		
185	40	331	73	Portland	
135	11	390	20	49	Wells

By Car

The good road conditions and inexpensive gas (compared to Europe and Canada) make getting around by car the best way to see the coast of Maine at your own pace. Good road maps are widely available in travel bookshops or, once you arrive, in gas stations. If you choose to rent a car, remember that several companies require you to be at least 25 years of age and to hold a major credit card.

Things to Consider

Driver's License: As a general rule, foreign drivers' licenses are valid in the United States. Take note that certain states are linked by computer to provincial police services in Canada and that a ticket issued in the United States is automatically transferred to your file in Canada.

Driving and the Highway Code: Signs marked "Stop" in white against a red background must always be respected. Some stop signs are accompanied by a small sign indicating "4-way". This means that all vehicles must stop at the intersection. Come to a complete stop even if there is no apparent danger. If two vehicles arrive at the same time, the one to the right has right of way. Otherwise the first car at the intersection has the right of way.

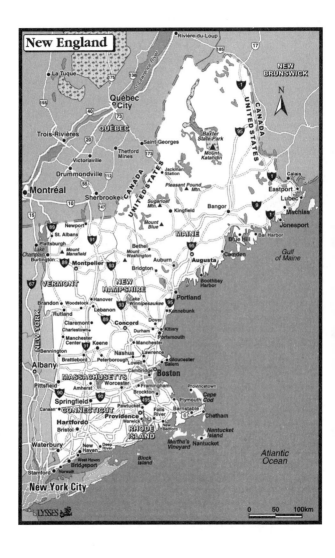

Traffic lights are often located on the opposite side of the intersection, so be careful to stop at the stop line, a white line on the pavement before the intersection.

Turning right on a red light after a full stop is permitted, unless otherwise indicated.

When a school bus (usually yellow) has stopped and has its signals flashing, you must come to a complete stop, no matter what direction you are travelling in. Failing to stop at the flashing signals is considered a serious offense, and carries a heavy penalty.

Seat belts must be worn at all times.

There are no tolls on the smaller highways and routes. Interstate 95, the Maine Turnpike is a toll highway. Interstate highways are indicated by a blue crest on a white background. The highway number and the state are written on the sign. "Interstate" is written on a red background at the top of the sign.

The speed limit is 55mph (88kph) on most highways. These signs are rectangular with a black border, white background and black writing.

Red and white triangular signs with the word "Yield" under them indicate that vehicles crossing your path have the right of way.

A round, yellow sign with a black X and two Rs indicates a railroad crossing.

Gas Stations: Because the United States produces its own crude oil, gasoline (petrol) prices are less expensive than in Europe; gas is also less expensive than in Canada, due to hidden taxes north of the border. Self-serve stations will often ask for payment in advance as a security measure

---

By Bus

After the car, the bus is the most efficient way of getting around. Well organized and inexpensive, buses cover most of Maine.

For information on schedules and destinations, contact your local Greyhound office.

Canadians can reserve tickets on Greyhound buses through Voyageur in Québec (Montréal: ☎ 514-842-2281) or through Greyhound in the rest of Canada (Toronto: ☎ 416-393-7911). Buses to Maine from destinations in Canada head first to Boston and from there into Maine, making for a fairly long trip.

Smoking is forbidden on most routes. In general, children under five travel for free. Passengers over 60 are eligible for considerable discounts. Animals are forbidden.

By Train

It is no longer possible to take the train to Maine. Amtrak, however, does offer connections by bus from Boston.

By Bicycle

Cyclists would do well to stick to the secondary roads. There are many of these up and down the coast of Maine.

INSURANCE

Cancellation Insurance

Your travel agent will usually offer you cancellation insurance when you buy your airline ticket or vacation package. This insurance allows you to be reimbursed for the ticket or package deal if your trip must be cancelled due to serious illness or death. Healthy people are unlikely to need this protection, which is therefore only of relative use.

Theft Insurance

Most residential insurance policies protect some of your goods from theft, even if the theft occurs in a foreign country. To make a claim, you must fill out a police report. It may not be necessary to take out further insurance, depending on the amount covered by your current home policy. As policies vary considerably, you are advised to check with your insurance company. European visitors should take out baggage insurance.

Life Insurance

Several airline companies offer a life insurance plan included in the price of the airplane ticket. However, many travellers already have this type of insurance and do not require additional coverage.

Health Insurance

This is the most useful kind of insurance for travellers, and should be purchased before your departure. Your insurance plan should be as complete as possible because health care costs add up quickly. When buying insurance, make sure it covers all types of medical costs, such as hospitalization, nursing services and doctor's fees. Make sure your limit is high enough, as these expenses can be costly. A repatriation clause is also vital in case the required care is not available on site. Furthermore, since you may have to pay immediately, check your policy to see what provisions it includes for such a situation. To avoid any problems during your vacation, always keep proof of your insurance policy on your person.

HEALTH

General Information

Vaccinations are not necessary for people coming from Europe or Canada. On the other hand, it is strongly suggested, particularly for medium or long-term stays, that visitors take out health and accident insurance. There are different types, so it is best to shop around. Bring along all medication, especially prescription medicine. Unless otherwise stated, the water is potable throughout Maine.

Be careful of the sun. The beaches of Maine are often fairly breezy places, and you might not realize you are getting a sun burn. Always use sunscreen with a minimum SPF of 15.

Safety

As with any area frequented by large numbers of tourists, travellers should watch out for themselves. By taking the necessary precautions, there is no reason to worry about your safety. If, however, you are unlucky, remember to dial **911** or **0** for the operator.

MONEY AND BANKS

Money

The monetary unit is the dollar ($), which is divided into cents (¢). One dollar = 100 cents.

Bills come in one, five, 10, 20, 50 and 100 dollar denominations; and coins come in one- (penny), five- (nickel), 10- (dime) and 25-cent (quarter) pieces. Dollar and fifty-cent coins exist, as does a two-dollar bill, but they are very rarely used.

Virtually all purchases must be paid in American currency in the United States. Be sure to get your travellers' cheques in American dollars. **Please note that all prices in this guide are in American dollars.**

Banks

Banks are open Monday to Friday from 9am to 3pm.

Banks can be found almost everywhere, and most offer the standard services to tourists. Most automatic teller machines (ATMs) accept foreign bank cards so that you can withdraw directly from your account (check before to make sure you have access) and avoid the potentially high charges of using a real teller. Most machines are open at all times. Cash advances on your credit card are another option, although interest charges accumulate quickly. Money orders are a final alternative for which no commission is charged. This option does, however, take more time. The easiest and safest way to carry your money, however, remains travellers' cheques.

Exchange Rates			
$1 CAN	= $0.71 US	$1 US =	$1.40 CAN
1 £	= $1.62 US	$1 US =	0.62 £
$1 Aust	= $0.81 US	$1 US =	$1.24 Aust
$1 NZ	= $0.69 US	$1 US =	$1.44 NZ
1 guilder	= $0.53 US	$1 US =	1.88 guilders
1 SF	= $0.70 US	$1 US =	1.43 SF
10 BF	= $0.29 US	$1 US =	35 BF
1 DM	= $0.57 US	$1 US =	1.74 DM
100 pesetas	= $0.72 US	$1 US =	140 pesetas
1000 lire	= $0.61 US	$1 US =	1637 lire

Exchanging Money

Several banks readily exchange foreign currency, but almost all charge a **commission**. There are exchange offices, on the other hand, that do not charge commission, but their rates are sometimes less competitive. These offices often have longer opening hours. It is a good idea to **shop around.**

Credit Cards

Most credit cards are accepted at stores, restaurants and hotels. While the main advantage of credit cards is that they allow visitors to avoid carrying large sums of money, using a credit card also makes leaving a deposit for a car-rental much easier and some cards, gold cards for example, automatically insure you when you rent a car. In addition, the exchange rate with a credit card is generally better. The most commonly accepted credit cards are Visa, MasterCard, American Express, Interbank, Barclay Bank, Diners' Club and Discovery.

BUSINESS HOURS AND PUBLIC HOLIDAYS

Business Hours

Stores are generally open from Monday to Saturday from 9:30am to 5:30pm (sometimes until 6pm). Supermarkets are usually open later, or in some places they are open 24 hours a day, seven days a week. Factory outlet stores keep much longer hours, and in some cases (L.L. Bean, for example) are open 24 hours a day, 365 days a year.

Public Holidays

The following is a list of public holidays in the United States. Most stores, administrative offices and banks are closed on these days.

New Year's Day (January 1)
Martin Luther King, Jr.'s Birthday (third Monday in January)
President's Day (third Monday in February)
Memorial Day (last Monday in May)
Independence Day (July 4)
Labor Day (first Monday in September)

Columbus Day (second Monday in October)
Veterans' Day (November 11)
Thanksgiving (fourth Thursday in November)
Christmas (December 25)

 ## ACCOMMODATIONS

The classic bed & breakfast is perhaps best exemplified in New England, and the coast of Maine is dotted with historic farmhouses and sea captains' houses that have been converted into bed & breakfasts. Not necessarily architecturally remarkable, these houses are quaint and cosy, have fireplaces, libraries and sometimes a friendly cat to redeem them. B&B organizations can provide listings of such establishments as well as of guesthouses, private homes with an extra room. When reserving be sure to inquire about the size of the B&B and the kind of accommodations it offers.

Among the other types of accommodation available, you have the choice between family motels, hotel chains, rustic cottages or grand houses by the sea where you'll be awakened by the cries of seagulls and the sound of waves lapping.

No matter what your budget or preferences, this guide has a place for you to lay your head. Remember that rooms are harder to come by and are more expensive in summer.

Note that many large hotels offer vacation and weekend packages, and that prices drop considerably during the off-season.

The "Accommodations" chapter in this guide presents a vast selection of hotels, organized by town and by price, from the least expensive to the most expensive. The prices given are those for the high season (summer); therefore, if you are planning to visit during another period of the year, ask about reductions. Prices are for one room, double occupancy.

Budget hotels *(less than $75 per night)* are usually clean, satisfactory but very modest. The advantages of mid-range hotels *($75 to $110)* vary with their location, though the rooms are generally larger. Those in the mid-to-high range *($110 to $150)* offer spacious rooms, attractive lobbies; most have restaurants, shops and a bar. Finally, luxury hotels *(more than $150)*, are the most prestigious in the region; besides all the facilities you'd expect from such an establishment, you'll find other perks like whirlpool baths, exercise rooms, 24-hour room service and gourmet dining.

If you've been dreaming of a room overlooking the sea, be sure to reserve well in advance. Remember that "oceanside" does not necessarily mean right on the beach. If you'd like to save some money, look for a place located two or three streets from the beach; the prices will almost always be smaller, and the money you'll save will make that extra walk to the beach worth it.

Renting a House

As rental information is constantly changing, it is impossible to list all the houses for rent. Nevertheless, this type of lodging is very popular in the region. Prices depend on the size of the house, how comfortable it is, the location, the season and the number of people. For complete information on the different agencies that specialize in rentals contact the chambers of commerce (see p 22).

 ## RESTAURANTS

Succulent dishes of local fish and seafood are the headliners at most restaurants on the Maine coast — from lobster to creamy clam chowder, and don't forget tender scallops, cod and mussels.

Besides seafood and traditional American cuisine, Maine's restaurants also serve a smorgasbord of different ethnic foods, as well as gourmet cuisine and fast-food. Whatever your preference or your budget, you'll find something to please your stomach.

The "Restaurants" chapter contains descriptions of restaurants organized by town and by price, from the least to the most expensive. At the least expensive places *($)*, where the bill should come to no more than about $8 (complete meal for one person not including drinks and tip), the atmosphere is informal, the service quick and the clientele local. In mid-range restaurants *($$)*, where a meal will still only cost you between $8 and $16, the ambiance is more relaxed, the menu more varied and the pace slower. At high-end restaurants *($$$)*, where you can eat for $16 to $24, the cuisine can be simple or elaborate, but the decor is more attractive and the service more personal. Finally, there are the luxury restaurants *($$$$)*, where prices start at $24. At these places, which often cater to gourmets, cooking becomes an art and the service is always impeccable.

Some restaurants close in winter.

When it comes to breakfast and lunch, prices vary less from one restaurant to another. Even mid-range to luxury restaurants usually offer breakfast and lunch specials that are only slightly more expensive than their budget counterparts. What's more, breakfast and lunch is a perfect opportunity to check out these ritzier places.

$	less than $8
$$	between $8 and $16
$$$	between $16 and $24
$$$$	more than $24

Tipping

In general, tipping applies to all table service (no tipping in fast-food restaurants). The tip is usually about 15% of the bill before tax, but varies, of course, depending on the quality of service. The tip is not included in the bill; you must calculate it yourself and leave it on the table for the waiter or waitress.

 # ENTERTAINMENT

Bars and Discotheques

Some establishments charge an entrance fee, especially when there is a band. Tipping is not obligatory, but it is appreciated;

if you do decide to tip, 10% to 15% is the norm. The legal drinking age is 21.

TRAVELLING WITH CHILDREN

All sorts of family adventures await you on the coast of Maine. Besides the many museums that cater to children, the region also boasts hundreds of beaches and amusement parks, as well as several parks that organize activities all year round.

Many bed & breakfasts don't accept children so be sure to ask when making your reservations. Also if you need a crib or a small bed, request it beforehand.

If you are travelling by car, bring water and juice, snacks and a few travel games. Always allow for more travelling time than you think you'll need, especially if you are taking secondary roads.

Remember that stores do not stay open as late in rural areas, so if you run out of diapers or baby food on the road you might have to make a big detour. To avoid this bring more of everything. In urban areas, keep an eye out for Store 24 or 7-11, both are usually open late or 24 hours a day.

SENIOR CITIZENS

In Maine, those aged 65 and older can take advantage of substantial reductions on admission prices to some museums and attractions, as well as special rates in some hotels, restaurants, etc. These special prices are often not advertised, so be sure to inquire.

The **American Association of Retired Persons (AARP)** *(601 E. Street NW, Washington,DC 20049, ☎ 202-434-2277)* accepts as members anyone over 50 who makes a request. This association offers several benefits to its members, including reduction on trips organized by various companies. Cruises and guided tours are available from the **AARP Travel Service** *(400 Pinnacle Way, Suite 450, Norcross, GA 30071, ☎ 1-800-927-0111)*.

When it comes to your health, be particularly careful. Besides your regular medications, also bring along your prescription in case you need to renew it. You might also consider bringing along your medical file, along with the name, address and telephone number of your doctor. Finally, make sure that your health insurance covers you while abroad.

DISABLED TRAVELLERS

Establishments throughout Maine are trying to make the most buildings possible accessible to disabled individuals. Most places have special wheelchair parking spaces, though few buses can accommodate wheelchairs.

The following American organizations can also provide useful information for disabled travellers: **Society for the Advancement of Travel for the Handicapped** *(347 5th Avenue, Suite 610, New York, NY 10016, ☎ 212-447-7284)*, **Travel Information SERVICE** *(Philadelphia, PA ☎ 212-456-9600)*, **Mobility International USA** *(P.O. Box 10767, Eugene OR 97440, ☎ 503-343-1284)* and **Flying Wheels Travel** *(P.O. Box 382, Owatonna, MN 55060, ☎ 1-800-535-6790)*. **Travelin' Talk** *(P.O. Box 3534, Clarksville, TN 37043, ☎ 615-552-6670)* regroups various networks offering similar information.

MISCELLANEOUS

Time Difference

Maine is on Eastern Standard Time, which is five hours behind Greenwich Mean Time. When it is noon in Portland it is also noon in New York and Montréal, 9am in Los Angeles and Vancouver, 5pm in London and 6pm in Paris.

Drugs

The United States has a strict policy on drugs (even "soft" drugs). Drug users and dealers caught with drugs in their possession risk severe consequences.

Electricity

Voltage is 110 volts throughout the United States, as in Canada. Electrical plugs are two-pinned and flat. Visitors from outside North America will need a transformer and a plug adapter. These are available here.

Weights and Measures

The United States use the imperial system:

Weights
1 pound (lb) = 454 grams (g)
1 kilogram (kg) = 2.2 pounds (lbs)

Linear Measure
1 inch = 2.2 centimetres (cm)
1 foot (ft) = 30 centimetres (cm)
1 mile = 1.6 kilometres (km)
1 kilometres (km) = 0.63 miles
1 metre (m) = 39.37 inches

Land Measure
1 acre = 0.4 hectare
1 hectare = 2.471 acres

Volume Measure
1 U.S. gallon (gal) = 3.79 litres
1 U.S. gallon (gal) = 0.83 imperial gallon

Temperature
To convert °F into °C: subtract 32, divide by 9, multiply by 5
To convert °C into °F: multiply by 9, divide by 5, add 32

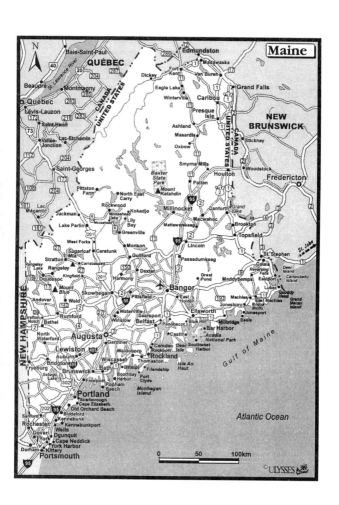

EXPLORING

The following chapter contains descriptions of all the attractions along the southearn coast of Maine between Kittery and Freeport. These are grouped by town and by tour on Highway 1, from south to north. Visitors will discover a rich culture and friendly people who take pride in their heritage. Let yourself be swept away by the beauty of the coast and all the deserted sandy beaches tucked away in its bays. Leave the daily grind behind as you awaken to the sound of waves lapping on shore and to the sight of the sun rising over the horizon.

This region has something for everyone. Architecture buffs will enjoy roaming the streets of York, Kennebunk and Portland. All sorts of fun awaits little children, who, after a session of sandcastle-building, will have little trouble finding something to amuse them. Nature-lovers seeking a good spot for a breath of fresh air will find just what they're looking for at Cape Elizabeth Park and on the Marginal Way in Ogunquit. The coast of Maine is full of surprises, so pack your sunglasses and head for "vacationland"!

 KITTERY ★

On Highway 4, Kittery is the first town you'll come to in Maine immediately after crossing the Piscataqua River.

Founded in 1647 on the banks of the Piscataqua River, Kittery quickly established itself as an important shipbuilding town, and the British built numerous military vessels here until 1776. The following year, the *Ranger* set out across the Atlantic from this little town in Maine to report Burgoyne's defeat to the French. In France, the boat received the first salute to the American flag, a first for a foreign war ship. The *Ranger* then headed back home, flying different flags in order to fool the British and thus further the American war effort. Despite all this, it was captured by the English, who thus incorporated it into their fleet.

Kittery's shipbuilding industry continued to flourish after the American Revolution. In 1800, the U.S. navy inaugurated the Portsmouth Naval Shipyard, a sizeable facility to this day.

It was also from Kittery, in 1745, that Sir William Pepperrell, the wealthiest landowner in Maine, set out at the head of a squadron of Englishmen and Americans to defeat the French in Louisbourg. This exploit earned him the title of baronet, a first for a native of the colony. Pepperrell succeeded in convincing his compatriots that it was possible to defeat the big European armies, a lesson that the Americans would not forget during the Revolution of 1776.

The **Kittery Historical and Naval Museum** *($3; May to Oct, every day 10am to 4pm; Rodgers Road, near Highways 1 and 236, ☎ 439-3080)* looks back on the evolution of shipyards in this region and elsewhere in the United States, and tells the history of this part of America. Visitors will find models of ships from the 18th century to the present day, as well as slide shows, photographs and paintings. The museum occasionally hosts special exhibitions as well.

Continue on Rodgers Road to Highway 103, which becomes Pepperrell's Road at Kittery Point. This part of town was one of the first areas of New England to be inhabited. It also offers an outstanding panoramic view out over Kittery Harbor.

Lady Pepperrell's Mansion *(private property; open to the public several days a year; inquire at the chamber of commerce, ☎ 439-7545 or 1-800-639-9645)*, overlooking the Piscataqua River, was erected in 1760, one year after Sir William Pepperell's death. Classical in style, it was modelled on Longfellow's Craigie House in Cambridge.

Continue on Highway 103. Fort McClary will be on your right, on Kittery Point Road.

Fort McClary ★ *(free admission; June to Sep, 9am to 5pm; Kittery Point Road, ☎ 439-2845)* stands in the oldest part of town. Kittery Point was fortified in the early 18th century to protect the town from the French, the natives and pirates. The oldest section of the fort was originally named Fort William, after Sir William Pepperell, a highly respected local aristocrat. During the War of Independence, the Americans enlarged the fort and established a garrison here. At that point, Fort William was renamed Fort McClary in memory of Major Andrew McClary, who had been killed at Bunker Hill. The English deemed the fort too well guarded to risk attacking. Fort McClary housed soldiers again in 1812; during the American Civil War; during the war against Spain and finally during World War I. This little state park, with its magnificent view of Kittery Harbor, is a wonderful spot for a family picnic.

Take Highway 1 to York.

 # YORK VILLAGE

Located on the banks of the York River since 1630, the village of York boasts a splendid historical quarter that merits a detour. Founded by Sir Ferdinand Gorges under the name "Gorgeana", York was the capital of the "Province of Mayne".

His plans for Maine having fallen through, Gorges abandoned the then capital in 1652. Gorgeana subsequently adopted the name York, in honour of one of Cromwell's celebrated victories in England, and established itself as an important shipbuilding centre. The town went through a trying time in the years following the Civil War, and only regained its former glory at the beginning of this century, when it became a choice summer vacation spot.

Old York is also famous for having put up a fierce resistance to the French and the natives. The Logg Garrison Houses that enabled local residents to defend themselves are still standing. A good example of these barracks is the **MacIntire Garrison** *(closed to the public; Highway 91)*, with its protruding third floor. The various Logg Garrison Houses, adaptations of a European style of wooden building, have spawned many a local stoyry. Legend has it that when the natives or French attacked, the women would pour boiling water on the enemy while the men pulled out their muskets. The MacIntire Garrison itself was built in 1707 according to the architectural tradition of the 17th century. The walls are 20 centimetres thick and covered with clapboards, giving the pseudo-military structure a massive, impregnable look.

The **Old York Historical Society** ★ *(207 York Street, ☎ 363-4974)* looks after seven 18th-century buildings. It has a lovely collection of furniture, fabrics and books once owned by the village's first families. These items are on view in the main building, the **George Marshall Store**, a former general store overlooking the town wharf.

Erected in 1750 for Captain Samuel Jefferds, **Jefferds Tavern** *($6; mid-June to Sep, 9am to 5pm; 1A Lindsay Road)* was a stopping place along the road between York and Kennebunk for many years. Today, it is the starting point of your tour, and houses a visitor's centre where you can learn about local history. The admission fee covers all seven of the Old York Historical Society's buildings.

The **Old Schoolhouse**, a small, one-room building attractively furnished with its original desks and chairs, presents a brief historical overview of the region's first schools.

One of the oldest public buildings in the United States, the **Old York Gaol** ★★ was once a royal prison for the district of Maine. This jail, whose walls are over one metre thick, was subsequently enlarged to make room for other cells and the guard's rooms before being closed down in 1860. A tour of the building is sure to give you the shivers. The judicial system in those days enabled any creditor to have another person incarcerated for non-payment of debt. This little prison was thus a place of misery for any number of farmers, who, in addition to being up to their ears in debt, found themselves separated from their family and locked up. You can also visit the guard's rooms, furnished in the style of 1790.

Since its construction in 1742, the **Emerson-Wilcox House** has been used for several different purposes. It was originally a post office, then a tavern and then a hairdressing salon, and then became a private home until finally being converted into a museum of local history. It displays various vestiges of the region's past.

The architecture along the coast of Maine is very distinctive. At the end of the 19th century, well-heeled Bostonians sought to revive the aesthetic qualities that had characterized New England in the previous century. They lamented the ugliness of their region and accused the new arrivals of ruining "their" New England. As Massachusetts was already a lost cause in their eyes, they chose Maine as the laboratory for what would come to be known as the Colonial Revival style. A good example of this style is the **Elizabeth-Perkins House** *(Lindsay Road)*. Instead of following the prevailing trend and building a luxurious home on York Harbor, Elizabeth Perkins decided to restore a simple house on the banks of the river, and succeeded in turning it into a model of the Colonial Revival style. Particularly noteworthy are its attractive kitchen and beams. This house became a sort of cultural centre for the region's summer residents.

The **John Hancock Warehouse** was built in the mid-18th century. Hancock was a wealthy merchant, as well as a patriot and the first person to sign the Declaration of Independence. Here, visitors can learn about the history of shipping in this region.

Take Maine Street to York Harbor

 # YORK HARBOR ★★

Crafts people selling their work are plentiful in this little harbour. You can stroll about at your leisure, falling in step with a different pace of life. You'll also find some superb houses, most built in the 19th century by Bostonians and New Yorkers looking to escape their usual urban environment.

In the 1760s, merchant Jonathan Sayward purchased a classical-style house dating from 1718. He enlarged it and decorated it with Queen Anne and Chippendale furniture. Legend has it that this furniture was plundered from the French at Louisbourg in 1745. Fortunately, the following generations kept the house and its furnishings intact. The **Sayward-Wheeler House** *(50-min guided tour; Jun to mid-Oct, Wed to Sun noon to 4pm; 79 Barell Lane Extension, ☎ 436-3205)* belongs to the Society for the Preservation of Historic Landmarks. The building itself is of little interest, but its decor is quite something. With its low ceilings, indicating that this was originally a modest home, this beautifully decorated house is an excellent example of the wealth accumulated by British colonists on the eve of the American Revolution.

Beaches

The little **York Harbor Beach** ★ is charming and intimate. Located in an attractive bay, it has fine sand, which makes for a soft bed on those days when the weather is just a little too hot. Being so tiny, it does not attract big crowds. Limited parking.

Take Long Beach Avenue to York Beach.

YORK BEACH

York Beach is only a few kilometres from York Village, but feels galaxies away. Things move at a slower and more traditional tempo in York Village and York Harbor, while York Beach is more popular, more rock 'n' roll. It is home to a hodgepodge of restaurants and souvenir shops, as well as a long row of hotels that stand like so many soldiers guarding the sea.

Two attractions dominate the landscape from the beach: **Mount Agamenticus** and the Nubble Light. Several hundred metres high (692 m), little Mount Agamenticus offers a magnificent view of the Presidential Range and the Gulf of Maine. For many years, it was an important landmark for sailors, as it stands out from the rest of the coastal plain.

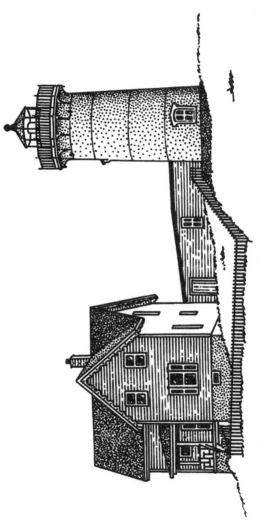

The Nubble Light

Get off of Highway 1A and take Nubble Road to the tip of Cape Neddick.

To this day, the **Nubble Light** ★, located on Cape Neddick, not only guides ships passing through the region, but is also a superb spot for shutterbugs. There is nothing extraordinary about the lighthouse itself, but the view of the Atlantic is worth the trip.

York's Wild Kingdom *(adults $11.50, children 10 and under $9.50; rides open from Jun to Labour Day, noon to 10pm; zoo open from May to Columbus Day, 10am to 5pm)* is a combination zoo and amusement park. Nearly 500 animals live here, and there are elephant and pony rides for the kids.

Beaches

The magnificent **Long Sands Beach** has rightfully established itself as the jewel of York. This 3.2-kilometre beach, which runs alongside the street of the same name, attracts crowds of summer visitors each year. While York Harbor Beach is quiet and intimate, Long Sand Beach is buzzing with activity. Don't worry, though: there's room for everyone. Here, too, however, the parking is limited.

Short Sands Beach, on the other side of Cape Neddick, is a miniature version of Long Sands Beach. The Victorian houses facing onto it lend it an atmosphere much appreciated by beach-goers—an added bonus to the pleasures of the sea. Furthermore, the busiest part of York, with its bars, restaurants and cafes, lies near Short Sands Beach.

Take Highway 1A back to Highway 1 and continue to Ogunquit.

OGUNQUIT ★★

"Ogunquit" is an Algonquian word meaning "a beautiful place near the sea". Modern-day artists agree wholeheartedly with this description. Indeed, Ogunquit became famous for the flurry of artistic activity that took place here at the beginning of the century. To this day, many people use their talents as landscape painters and writers to immortalize this long, powdery beach. As a result, Ogunquit abounds in art galleries and craft shops where you can while away a rainy afternoon, or even spend a delightful summer evening. Ogunquit is also a favourite vacation spot among the gay community—the most popular U.S. destination after Provincetown.

Ogunquit has managed to preserve its picturesque appearance in spite of the growing numbers of tourists that flock here. The beach has been protected, thanks to some clever and effective town planning, which has kept the parking lots at a good distance. It does the soul good to relax here, far from the noise and pollution of cars. A stroll along the Marginal Way (see p 78) on a warm summer night is always a treat.

Buses that look like old-time streetcars carry visitors to the major points of interest. This ingenious mode of transportation helps prevent traffic backups on the streets of the little village.

In keeping with its reputation as an artists' colony, Ogunquit has built itself a lovely little **Museum of American Art ★** *(adults $3, seniors $2, free admission for children under 12; Jun to Sep, Mon to Sat 10:30am to 5pm, Sun 2pm to 5pm; Shore Road, ☎ 646-4909)*, which exhibits pieces by artists who are presently working in the region or have done so in the past. An impressive number of windows lends the museum a distinctive charm and brightness and also provides museum-goers with a constant view of the sea. Finally, in addition to temporary exhibitions of nationally renowned works, the museum displays some magnificent oils by Henry Strater, among others.

The **Barn Gallery** *(Jun to Sep, Mon to Sat 10am to 5pm, Sun 2pm to 5pm; ☎ 646-5370)*, of a more modest size than the Museum of American Art, exhibits works by members of the Ogunquit Art Association. It frequently presents conferences, films and even concerts.

 Beaches

Ogunquit's main beach is divided into two vaguely defined sections, **Main Beach ★** and **Footbridge Beach**. Both are pleasant but crowded. They are located just a few minutes from the centre of town and are open from 8am to 5pm during the summer. These public beaches came at a high price. In 1820, Charles Tibbetts, a New Hampshire native, purchased the land on which Ogunquit Beach lies. When the delegates of the Ogunquit Village Corporation learned that Tibbetts wanted to sell the land to an amusement park company, they cancelled the deal. To do so, they went to Augusta, the state capital, to request permission to turn the beach into a public park, and won their battle fairly easily. They then established the Ogunquit Beach District, imposing a supplementary tax on local residents in order to raise the $43,500 necessary to maintain the beach. The Corporation's primary goal was to prevent any construction here, which explains why the beach is in such good shape.

Near the **Beach Street** entrance, you'll find restaurants, toilets and a parking lot ($2 per hour). Footbridge Beach *(at the end of Ocean Street)*, for its part, only offers parking, but is much less crowded.

Take Shore Road to Perkins Cove or walk there on the Marginal Way. It is almost impossible to park in Perkins Cove during summer, but you can always take the streetcar.

 PERKINS COVE

This little hamlet is actually Ogunquit's port. In the 1930s, it became clear that the little cove reserved for fishermen and water sports fans was too narrow. The fishermen joined forces, and the Perkins Cove Harbor Project was born. The bay was thus enlarged to its present size. Today, Perkins Cove is a small fishing village boasting charming art shops, restaurants and cafes. You can stroll about between the fine restaurants and the peaceful outdoor seating areas. There is a pedestrian footbridge linking the two sides of the cove. When a boat approaches the port, it blows its whistle three times to signal the harbour master to raise the bridge, which splits into two unequal parts; the longer opens mechanically, the shorter manually. The summer crowds make parking almost impossible, so you are better off either taking the streetcar or walking here along the magnificent Marginal Way.

Take Highway 1 to Wells.

WELLS

Wells is a little town sandwiched between Highway 1A and the sea. Its long beach is connected to Ogunquit's by Moody Beach. Wells Beach is semi-private, which means that it can only be used by people who own or rent one of the numerous houses along it. If you want to enjoy the surf and sand here, you'll have to rent a house or a room with access to the beach. The centre of town lies on the other side of Highway 1. This area is known for its shops, particularly its antique dealers. Wells is said to be a paradise for people looking for antiques and old books. Bargains are rare here, though.

The **Wells Auto Museum** *($3.50; mid-June to Sep 10am to 5pm, May to mid-Jun and early Oct Sat and Sun 10am to 5pm; Highway 1, ☎ 646-9064)* has a collection of over 70 old cars and motorcycles. Unless you're a car fanatic, this place will be of little interest to you.

 Beaches

Moody Beach *(Highway 1, then Eldrige Street)* is the continuation of Ogunquit Beach, and it, too, is very pleasant, a place where sun-worshipping summer visitors come looking for a little ocean blue. Bear in mind that you have to head right once you get on the beach, since the other side is private.

Wells Beach is the east end of the long strip of fine sand leading to the towns of Ogunquit and Wells. The beach is wide and smooth. It's a great place for body-surfing. Nearby, you'll find public rest rooms, a few shops, restaurants, a casino, etc. Parking costs $6 a day.

Take Highway 1 several kilometres farther to Kennebunk.

 KENNEBUNK ★★

Kennebunk used to have a large shipyard, and the local captains and shipbuilders built magnificent homes here. These opulent houses reflect all the great American architectural traditions—Queen Anne, neoclassical, Federal, etc. Among the more noteworthy are the **James Smith Homestead** *(private; Highway 35)*, which will give you an idea of what a Georgian farmhouse might have been like, and the **Bourne Mansion** *(private; 8 Bourne Street)*, a fine example of the Federal style.

The Kennebunks

The villages of Kennebunk, Kennebunkport, Kennebunk Beach, Cape Porpoise and Arundel are known collectively as the Kennebunks. Newly famous as the location of former U.S. President George Bush's summer home, the area has actually been popular with vacationers ever since the 1870s. The Massachusetts-based Boston and Kennebunk Sea Shore Company purchased the land stretching from Lord's Point, at the west end of Kennebunk Beach, to Cape Porpoise, then built 30 large hotels and several dozen houses to accommodate the New Yorkers and Bostonians who flocked to the region each summer. The 1940s, 1950s and 1960s saw a decline in the Kennebunks' popularity, but the local tourist industry took off again in the 1970s, and has been growing continuously ever since. Several old hotels have been renovated, a series of B&Bs have opened up, and a whole slew of restaurants now attend to the pleasures of the palate.

Nowadays, the Kennebunks are one of the best destinations in Maine. The centre of Kennebunk lies right near the I-95 and just a 10-minute drive from the beach. The region is slightly less crowded than other vacation spots along the coast of Maine, and offers better restaurants and accommodations. The only drawback is that everything is more expensive here than at places like Ogunquit and Old Orchard.

You can also see the famous **Wedding Cake House ★** *(public access only to the little art gallery; Highway 9A)*. According to legend, the captain who owned this house had to rush off to sea shortly before his wedding. The ceremony took place, but there hadn't been enough time to make a cake beforehand. To cheer up his bride, the captain promised to have their house decorated like a cake. The real story is less romantic, however.

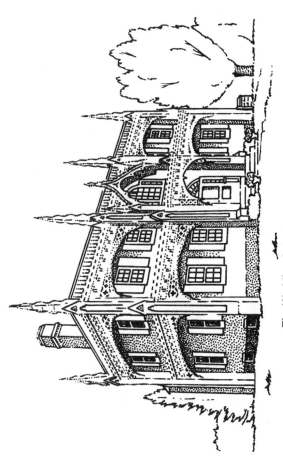

The Wedding Cake House

The owner at the time, George Bourne, had suffered several failures, both professionally and in his love life. He had been a wealthy shipbuilder for many years, but the local decline of that industry plunged him into bankruptcy. The size and extravagance of the project seems to have allowed him to forget about his setbacks for a little while. He finished the house in the summer of 1856 and died of typhoid fever in December of the same year.

The **Brick Store Museum** *($3; May to mid-Dec, Tue to Sat 10am to 4:30pm; Jan to Apr, Tue to Fri 10am to 4:30pm; 117 Main Street, ☎ 985-4802)* is a former general store. The ground floor houses an exhibition on the region's maritime and social history, while the second floor is devoted to a collection of Federal-style furniture, portraits and paintings of boats. Also on display are a number of objects once owned by Kenneth Roberts, famous for his novel *Arundel*, set in Kennebunk.

The Federal-style **Taylor-Barry House** *($2; Jun to Sep, Tue to Fri 1pm to 4pm or by appointment, inquire at the Brick Store Museum; 24 Summer Street, ☎ 985-4802)* belonged to a local captain. The period corridor and furniture are particularly noteworthy.

Take Highway 35 to Highway 9, then turn left toward Kennebunkport or continue straight ahead to Kennebunk Beach.

 # KENNEBUNKPORT ★★

Kennebunkport is now famous as the location of former U.S. President George Bush's summer residence, which has been in his family since the beginning of the century. Bush is not Kennebunkport's first famous resident, however. Author Kenneth Roberts was the first to introduce the region to the rest of the country in the 1920s and the 1930s. His descriptions of life in colonial America soon made him very popular. His novels *Rabble in Arms*, *Northwest Passage*, *Oliver Wiswell* and *Arundel* are precious sources of information on that era. The village of North Kennebunk even changed its name to Arundel as a tribute to the writer. Kenneth Roberts was a colourful character who wanted to isolate himself from civilization. His popularity and the public's growing interest in Kennebunkport nearly drove him mad. He was even seen

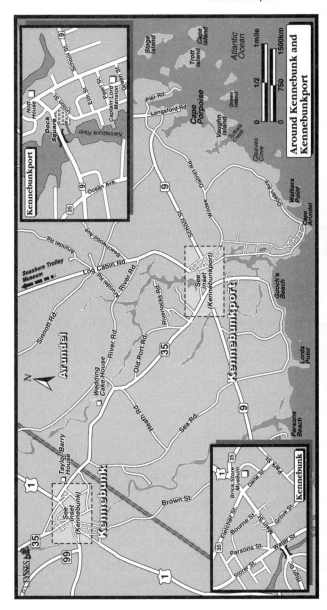

Around Kennebunk and Kennebunkport

shooting at an airplane once because he hated the noise so much. He ended up retiring to a more peaceful spot.

Kennebunkport, located on the banks of the Kennebunk River, was once home to a shipyard as well. Like Kennebunk, it has a rich historic neighbourhood with superb houses built in styles ranging from Georgian to Federal. In the late 19th century, the decline of the shipbuilding industry forced the town to shift over to tourism—a change for which the rest of us can only be grateful!

The centre of town, around **Dock Square**, is always bustling. The neighbouring streets are lined with all sorts of shops and art galleries, as well as a number of charming little restaurants. During summer, Dock Square is overrun by browsing tourists.

Take Spring Street to Maine Street and turn left.

Built in 1853 for Charles Perkins, the **Nott House** ★ *($3; Maine Street, ☎ 967-2751)* is a fine example of neoclassical architecture. Its Doric columns have earned it the name "White Columns". Perkins and his wife, Celia Nott Perkins, moved into the house after their wedding. A guided tour traces the history of both the couple and the house through Celia's private journal. The original decor still shines in all its glory.

Continue on Maine Street to Green Street, and walk down the latter for a block.

Now an inn, the **Captain Lord Mansion** ★ *(at the corner of Green and Pleasant)* is sure to catch your attention. Captain Nathaniel Lord built this house between 1812 and 1815. Its highly symmetrical design and front door, with its Palladian window, are hallmarks of the Federal style.

Retrace your steps and follow Maine Street to the end. Head north on North Street, which turns into Log Cabin Road, to the Seashore Trolley Museum.

The **Seashore Trolley Museum** ★ *($6; May to mid-Oct, every day 10am to 5:30pm; Log Cabin Road, ☎ 967-2800)* has rescued—and more importantly, restored—a large number of streetcars. Visitors will find over 225 of these vehicles from all over the world—from Boston and New York to Sydney and

Nagasaki. The short ride (approx. 5 km) along an old streetcar route is sure to be a hit with the kids. The trip includes a fascinating stop at the museum's repair shop, where heaps of metal are transformed into glorious souvenirs of the beginning of the century. Not to be missed.

 ## Beaches

To avoid being completely overrun by visitors on weekends, the town of Kennebunk requires parking permits *($5 per day, $15 per week, $30 per month)*. These are available at the police station in Kennebunk (not Kennebunkport); you can also get one at your hotel. This system has enabled the town to control the number of beach-goers and thereby keep the local beaches relatively peaceful.

The beaches are open in July and August from 9am to 5pm. With the special permit, you can park your car in the municipal lots. Still, the best way to get to the beach is to take the Trolley Bus, which runs all day long and will take you anywhere you want in town for just 50¢.

Kennebunkport is surrounded by three magnificent beaches. **Kennebunk Beach** *(along Beach Avenue)* stretches some three kilometres. Its three sections (Gooch's Beach, Middle Beach and Mother's Beach) form a lovely setting in which to relax. Part fine sand, part pebbles, this gorgeous beach is much less crowded than those in Ogunquit and Old Orchard. The sound of the endless sea is wonderfully soothing; if you listen closely, it will tell you the story of the men and women who built New England. **Gooch's Beach** and **Middle Beach** mainly attract adults in search of a peaceful spot to sunbathe. You'll also see a few surfers in the waves. **Mother's Beach ★** welcomes flocks of children, with mothers and fathers in tow. This little beach is ideal for families, as it is always easy to keep a watchful eye over children.

Take Highway 9 toward Wells.

Parson's Beach ★ is a haven of peace. Little known, this small beach offers simplicity, tranquillity and fine sand. You can stroll along it all alone at night in the pale moonlight. It should be noted that there is very little parking here. You should probably leave your car on Highway 9 and walk down maple-lined Grand Avenue to the beach.

Head east on the 9 to Dyke Road. Take the latter to King's Highway, then head west to Goose Rocks Beach.

 ## GOOSE ROCKS BEACH

This quiet little hamlet is a refuge for solitude-seekers. Here, you'll find a number of peaceful little houses looking out onto the Atlantic as if hypnotized by the power and the beauty of the vast ocean.

 ## Beaches

The beach at **Goose Rocks Beach** *(along King's Highway)* stretches a little farther than the others, north of the village of Kennebunkport. Wide and covered with fine sand, it offers magnificent views of the islands facing it. This beach is sure to appeal to walkers, who can marvel at the sun glinting off the ocean in the morning. The calm waters in the little bay make it popular with families, a bit like Mother's Beach. You'll need a special parking permit for this beach, too. It costs the same as the one for Kennebunk Beach, and is available at the Kennebunkport (not Kennebunk) police station.

From Kennebunkport, take Main Street to Highway 9 and head east to Pier Road, in the village of Cape Porpoise. Pier Road will take you to the town pier.

 ## CAPE PORPOISE ★★

At Cape Porpoise, you'll find a small bay with humble fishing boats moored in it. If you're looking for a tranquil spot where the picturesque side of Maine is alive and well, you're sure to be enchanted by this tiny village, founded by John Smith in the colony's earliest days. The local fishermen set the tempo for life here on the Cape. At dawn, they set out silently on the mirror-like water to haul up their cages, then bring lobster and crabs back to the ponds along the coast. Needless to say, Cape Porpoise enjoys a solid reputation among seafood lovers.

From Kennebunkport, take Highway 35 north to Highway 1, then head east to Saco.

 SACO

Saco is the little town that marks the start of Old Orchard Beach. Many of the residents trace their roots back to Québec, so you'll see French names on local signs (Tremblay Hardware Store, Pilon Insurance, etc.). According to U.S. statistics, there are over seven million Americans of French-Canadian origin. In the last century, Québec was hit by an economic crisis and huge numbers of people flooded out of the province in search of work. At the same time, the American textile industry was flourishing, and there was a labour shortage. Many Québec families thus abandoned their farms for the United States.

Today, Saco provides the necessary services for Old Orchard's summer visitors. A good number of tourist attractions aimed at children have sprung up along Highway 1, along with hotels, motels and restaurants that offer excellent value for travellers on a limited budget.

The **York Institute Museum** *(adults $2, under 16 $1; May to Oct, Tue to Fri 1pm to 4pm; Jul and Aug, Tue to Sat 1pm to 4pm; Nov to Apr, Tue and Wed 1pm to 4pm, Tue 1pm to 8pm during the rest of the year; 371 Main Street, ☎ 282-3031)* houses a collection of works related to the history of the southern coast of Maine. Visitors can view a selection of original paintings, furniture and tools. The museum also organizes conferences, excursions and special exhibitions.

The whole family will enjoy a trip to the **Maine Aquarium** *(adults $6; every day; ☎ 284-4511)*, where penguins, sharks and other marine creatures can be seen frolicking about. There are also picnic areas and short hiking trails on the grounds.

Also for the entire family, **Funtown USA** and **Cascade Water Park** *(mid-Jun to mid-Sep, weekends in spring and fall; Highway 1, at the corner of the I-95, ☎ 284-5139 or 287-6231)* offer classic amusement park entertainment, including thrilling water rides. The **Aquaboggan Water Park** *(Jun to Sep; Highway 1, ☎ 282-3112)* also welcomes fans of water rides and other forms of aquatic entertainment (aquaboggans, bumper boats, swimming pool, etc.).

From Saco, take Highway 5, which leads straight to Old Orchard Beach.

 OLD ORCHARD

The orchard after which this place was named was planted by one Thomas Roger in 1657. It wasn't until 1837, however, that Old Orchard's future as a tourist resort first took shape, thanks to a man named E.C. Staples, who built the first local hotel, Old Orchard House. In those days, Staples charged guests $1.50 a week. With the construction of the Grand Trunk Railway, American and Canadian travellers began flocking to Old Orchard and other spots along the coast of Maine.

Old Orchard has an almost infectious, carnival-like atmosphere. Scores of French-Canadians vacation here, carving out a place in the sun for themselves. You'll hear more French spoken here than anywhere else in the United States, aside from Florida. The region tends to get overcrowded, especially on hot summer days. Old Orchard is divided into two sections, the Pier and Ocean Park. The Pier is the liveliest section, where all the fast-food stands and bars are located, along with the miniature golf course (though the word "miniature" hardly applies!). **Ocean Park**, on the other side of Old Orchard Bay, is a bit quieter.

This area is a good choice for families and travellers on a limited budget, as it offers a wide selection of affordable hotels, motels and campgrounds. On the other hand, Old Orchard is a nightmare for anyone looking for solitude and peace and quiet.

The **Pier** is almost a local institution. The original structure, made entirely of iron, was built in 1898. There were several buildings on it, which housed a miniature zoo, a casino and a number of restaurants. The Pier was renovated several times, and then finally, in 1980, the town decided to build a new one. This time, the architects used wood as the primary material.

The Pier still has all sorts of facilities and services, including numerous restaurants, souvenir shops and even bars.

Even after 60 years, **Playland Palace** *(pay per ride (prices vary) or $16 for the afternoon; Jun to Sep; ☎ 934-2001)* still attracts crowds of thrill-seekers. It has a variety of children's games and rides, including a carrousel with hand-painted horses. For a magnificent view of the Saco harbour, take a ride on the Ferris wheel.

 Beaches

Old Orchard Beach ★ is without question one of the loveliest beaches on the entire Maine coast. Nearly four kilometres long, it is very wide and well maintained. Watch out for the tide, though; the water rises quickly in these parts. Unlike the stricter (read "snobbier") beaches in the Kennebunks, games and children are welcome here. In addition to the usual sand-castle architects, you'll also see people playing volleyball, "Olympic" frisbee and all sorts of other beach sports. The sweat you'll work up enjoying these activities will make the cold Atlantic waters bearable. No pets on the beach before 5pm.

Continue on Highway 1 to the 207 and head for Prouts Neck.

 PROUTS NECK ★

Prouts Neck is a small, oddly-shaped peninsula. It has a long white-sand beach that lies opposite Old Orchard Beach. This jutting promontory was immortalized by the great American artist Winslow Homer. After a successful career as a watercolour-painter, most notably during the Civil War, Homer went to Great Britain to study the lifestyle of the fishermen in the North Sea. There, he developed a passion for the confrontation between man and the sea, that never-ending battle between intelligence and sheer force.

In 1875, Homer and his brother came to Prouts Neck with the idea of building a summer home here for their family. They purchased almost the entire peninsula. As expected, Prouts

Neck became popular, and they sold off a few pieces of property, choosing their buyers very carefully. Winslow Homer loved solitude and isolation, not only in his studio, but also during his long walks along the shores of the bay.

Homer stayed on the peninsula for weeks after the summer visitors had left. He liked this time of the year, when autumn was approaching and the waves of the Atlantic reached 10 to 15 metres high. He drew inspiration from the power of the gigantic sea pounding against the rocky shore, saturating the air with the smell of sea salt. He would also watch the fishermen bringing in their last catches, their faces haggard from an arduous summer and the ocean winds.

In 1884, he switched from watercolours to oils. This weather-beaten but blessed coast and its inhabitants, both men and women, living in step with the tides, are featured in his paintings. His style is reminiscent of French impressionism, and his works convey a true passion for light and for capturing the moment. Among his most celebrated works are *The Life-line*, showing a woman being saved from a shipwreck, *The Fog Warning* and *Artist's Studio in an Afternoon Fog*, which won him international renown. He stopped painting in 1909, at the age of 73, and died the following year.

 Beaches

Prouts Neck is still an attractive vacation spot. It has three beaches. The first, which belongs to the **Prouts Neck Association**, is private. Day-passes are available at the Black Point Inn (see p 90), at the entrance to the beach. The inn also runs a restaurant and a small snack bar. If you're looking for a slightly more laid-back place to enjoy the surf and sand, the **Scarborough Beach ★** *(to the northeast, on Highway 207)* is just as elegant, but you'll have to bring along some picnic fixings, as there is no restaurant here. Scarborough Beach is small but rarely crowded, due to the limited parking. Finally, **Higgin's Beach** *(Highway 77)* is the most popular of the three, even though there is no parking at all.

Continue on Highway 1 to the 114 and head for Cape Elizabeth.

CAPE ELIZABETH ★

Towering over the Atlantic like an immortal guardian of silence, the **Portland Head Light** is the most oft-depicted symbol of Maine. George Washington himself ordered the construction of this lighthouse in 1790. Imagine the terror of a captain sailing toward this rugged coast on a foggy morning. Watch the surf violently pounding this coast and imagine what those rocks could do to the hull of a ship. There are panels on which visitors can read the story of the *Amie C. McGuire*, which ran aground on Christmas Eve, 1886. The little park surrounding the lighthouse is a perfect spot for a family picnic, and the lighthouse keeper's house now contains a pleasant little **museum** *(adults $2, children $1; Jun to Oct 10am to 4pm; Nov, Dec, Apr and May weekends 10am to 4pm; 1000 Shore Road, ☎ 799-2661)* on the American ship-building industry and the history of lighthouses around the world.

Crescent Beach State Park ★ *(adults $2.50, children 5 to 11, 50¢)* is another very popular site—this time with local inhabitants. The fine-sand beach is one of the loveliest in Maine, and has all the necessary facilities and services (restrooms, restaurants, etc.). As indicated by its name, **Two Lights State Park** *($1.50; Apr 15 to Nov)*, also on Cape Elizabeth, is laid out around two lighthouses. The Cape Elizabeth Light still guides boats passing through the area, while its twin retired several years ago. If you feel like it, you can climb to the top of the former military tower for a sweeping view of the Atlantic.

Take Highway 77, which leads to Portland.

 PORTLAND ★★★

Portland, a small city overlooking Casco Bay, is nicknamed the San Francisco of the East. Its narrow streets that seem to plunge into the sea, its scores of Victorian houses and its cultural scene, surprisingly vital for a town of only 65,000 inhabitants, are all reminiscent of San Francisco, but the comparison is still unfair. Portland has a soul of its own, the soul of a city with a rich and fascinating history, the soul of a city that has been burned and reconstructed, the soul of proud city that is now resolutely looking to the future.

Even in the early days of colonization, the French, English, natives and pirates were already crossing swords here. All four groups depended on the fur trade, the timber industry or fishing for their livelihood. In 1715, a battalion was sent here from Massachusetts to fortify the city. In 1770, the city was named Falmouth, and attained a certain level of prosperity thanks to the ship-building industry and the exportation of fur, wood and fish.

In October 1775, during the War of Independence, the British took up position in the harbour and set fire to the town, an event that stirred up a great deal of revolutionary sentiment in the 13 colonies. Even in ruins, Falmouth was too proud to give up. About a hundred colonists stayed here and rebuilt the city. On July 4, 1786, Falmouth was renamed Portland.

Portland gradually established itself as a major port on the East Coast, and thus enjoyed a period of affluence in the 19th century, especially in the ship-building, textile and lumber industries. The town had about a dozen shipyards, which built vessels for Russia, India and Europe. The first sugar refinery in the United States, the Portland Sugar Company, was also founded during this period.

During the Civil War, 5,000 local abolitionists joined President Lincoln's troops. Just after the conflict, in 1866, Portland was ravaged by flames once again; this time, nearly a third of the city was destroyed.

Fortunately, a few examples of the Portland's traditional architecture survived the fire of 1866, making a stroll through the city's historic quarter very interesting. One noteworthy building is the **Tate House (1)** *(adults $3, children $1; Jul to mid-Sep, Tue to Sat 10am to 4pm, Sun 1pm to 4pm; 1270 Westbrook Street, ☎ 774-9781)*, a magnificent example of the Georgian style built in 1755. George Tate, a forest inspector for the British Crown, lived here from 1755 to 1794. His son became the first American to attain the rank of admiral in the Russian navy.

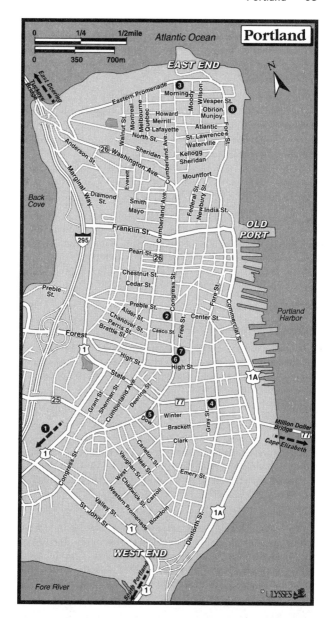

The **Wadsworth Longfellow House (2)** *(adults $3, children $1; Jun to Oct, Tue to Sat 10am to 4pm, closed July 4 and Labour Day; gallery and library open year round, Wed to Sat noon to 4pm; 485 Congress Street, ☎ 879-0427)*, built by the grandfather of the celebrated American poet, was the home of a very important Portland family: Peleg Wadsworth was a hero of the American Revolution and Henry Wadsworth Longfellow needs no further introduction. After the American Revolution, a good number of loyal British subjects had to leave the country, abandoning their jobs and any other sources of income. The Wadsworth and Longfellow families seized the opportunity to make a fortune themselves. The museum in the house traces the poet's childhood and points out the important role Portland has played in American culture.

You have to climb some 100 steps to reach the top of the **Portland Observatory (3)** *(adults $1.50, children 50¢; Jun, Sep and Oct, Fri to Sun 1pm to 5pm; Jul and Aug, Wed Thu and Sun 1pm to 5pm, Fri and Sat 10am to 5pm; 138 Congress Street, ☎ 772-5546)*, the only remaining observatory on the Atlantic coast. Imagine families waiting impatiently for ships to arrive, scanning the horizon over and over in the hope of catching sight of a sail in the distance. Built in 1807, this octagonal building offers an outstanding view of the sea.

The austere exterior of **Victoria Mansion (4)** *(adults $4, children $1.50; Jun to Sep, Tue to Sat 10am to 4pm, closed July 4 and Labour Day; Labour Day to Columbus Day, weekends noon to 4pm; 109 Danforth Street, ☎ 722-4841)* conceals all sorts of surprises; the ornamentation inside is extremely impressive. With its trompe l'œil frescoes, rich woodwork and marble, this home is one of the finest examples of the luxury of the 1850s. Designed by Henry Austin, it belonged to Rugles S. Morse, a Maine native who made a fortune in the hotel business in New Orleans. As Morse spent much of his time in Louisiana, he used his house in Portland very rarely, which explains why it is in such excellent condition.

In 1829, Neil Dow, the man later responsible for getting the first prohibition law in the United States ratified in Maine (1851), was leading quite a comfortable existence. His home, now the **Neil Dow Memorial (5)** *(every day 9am to 4pm; 714 Congress Street, ☎ 773-7773)* reflects the wealth he acquired as the Mayor of Portland and an officer in the

Portland

Northern Army. Neoclassical in style, this house is now maintained by the Maine Women's Christian Temperance Union.

Founded in 1882, the **Portland Museum of Art** ★★ **(6)** *(adults $3.50, children $1; Tue to Sat 10am to 5pm, Thu to 9pm, Sun noon to 5pm, closed New Year's Day, Christmas, July 4 and Thanksgiving Day; 7 Congress Street, ☎ 775-6148, 761-ARTS or 800-639-4067)* holds an impressive collection of works by American artists, including Winslow Homer. The Joan Whitney Payson collection, which became part of the museum's permanent collection in 1991, includes works by Degas, Renoir and even Picasso.

The **Children's Museum of Maine (7)** *(142 Free Street, ☎ 828-1234)* has several interactive children's games. The "Maine Street" exhibition includes playgrounds and activities for the very young. This is a good place for an afternoon of family fun.

From the 1870s to the 1940s, Maine was in a league of its own as far as the railroad was concerned; its rails, only 60 centimetres apart, were actually more economical than those used elsewhere. The train carried travellers to the most isolated parts of Maine. Unfortunately, the company that ran the railroad ended up going bankrupt. A millionaire with a passion for the local "two-footers" decided to purchase all the equipment and use it to create "Edaville", a major tourist attraction that shut down in 1991 after a disagreement regarding a lease. With the help of a few friends, Phineas Sprague, Jr. moved the locomotives to Portland, and the **Maine Narrow Gauge Railroad Co. & Museum (8)** *(every day 10am to 4pm; 58 Fore Street, ☎ 828-0814)* was born. The exhibition displays the key parts of the rail system: locomotives, cabooses and a Ford Model T transformed into an inspection vehicle. Visitors can also see a short video recreating the important events in the history of these trains.

Take the I-95 east to Freeport.

FREEPORT

This little town's name is now synonymous with shopping. For nearly 75 years, the L.L. Bean store has been serving outdoor enthusiasts around the clock, 365 days a year. A New England institution, this retailer has attracted not only consumers, but also a flock of other well-known stores, such as the Gap, Polo Ralph Lauren and Calvin Klein, to the area. Still, Freeport has more to offer than bargains.

This little town, located east of Portland, became an important shipping centre in the years following the Civil War. It then acquired a good reputation for its mackerel and, later, for its crabmeat. Finally, the centre of town boasts some beautifully preserved colonial architecture.

Many visitors are sure to be surprised by the **Desert of Maine** *(guided tour, adults $4.75, children $2,75, seniors $2.25; mid-May to mid-Oct, 9am to sunset; Desert Road, ☎ 865-6962)*, located a few kilometres outside of town. The site was originally a farm, which was converted into a lumberyard after its overworked soil became unproductive. As the ground eroded over the years, sand dating from the ice age surfaced—so much of it that entire trees were swallowed up! The mineral composition of the soil has made it unusable for commercial purposes. Guided tours are organized, and hikers can explore nearly 40 hectares of land. Visitors can also tour a small sand museum and even camp out here in the desert.

OUTDOORS

With the Atlantic lapping at its shores, Maine has much to offer outdoor enthusiasts. From swimming in the open sea to bird-watching, this chapter covers the major outdoor activities enjoyed on southern Maine coast. So, tie up your bootlaces, prepare your paddle, get your bathing suit on, and explore — in coastal Maine, all roads lead to the beach!

 ## SWIMMING

If you are accustomed to the warm seas of the Caribbean, Maine has a little surprise in store for you. In fact, the water temperature fluctuates between 12° C and 17° C, and rarely rises above 20° C. It is cold. That said, when the sun heats the beach to close to 35° C in the shade, a refreshing dip in the ocean becomes more appealing.

Although the water may be cold, Maine's beaches are beautiful. Imagine kilometres of soft sand shining with purple, orange, and yellow rays of morning sunlight. The beaches provide friendly meeting places for frisbee tournaments, beach ball olympics and classes in contemporary sandcastle architecture of the "Ogunquit School"...

Whether tucked into the nooks of bays, or simply braving the open sea, the beaches of Maine are, without exception, enchanting. Each beach and its facilities are described in detail in the "Exploring" chapter.

 # BIRD-WATCHING

Many organizations, such as Rachel Carson's National Wildlife Refuge, are working to create spaces where animals will be respected. The coast of Maine is home to many groups advocating the protection of marine reserves. Besides providing a habitat for aquatic animals, these areas serve as nesting grounds for an assortment of bird species.

Bird-watching enthusiasts will take pleasure in strolling along the trails that are maintained in these parks. Admittedly it's not the Amazon, but you can observe a variety of aquatic bird species, as well as flocks of migrating birds that stop over in spring and autumn.

Ogunquit

Wells National Estuarine Research Reserve at Laudholm Farm *(parking $5; every day 8am to 5pm; Laudholm Road, ☎ 646-1555)* is divided into two parts. The first, **Laudholm Farm**, an old estate belonging to the Lord family, is maintained as a nature education centre. It includes a small exhibition, a slide projection room, washrooms, and a parking lot. The birds that frequent this park have a bird's-eye view of 12 kilometres of walking trails departing from the farm. The second part, **Laudholm Trust**, offers basically the same experience by means of guided walking excursions. Arrive early in the morning, when the site is less crowded.

A little less impressive, mainly due to its location along Route 9, **Rachel Carson National Wildlife Refuge** *(free; from sunrise to sunset; Route 9, ☎ 646-9226)* offers a short, one-kilometre hike through pine-tree undergrowth interspersed with ponds. Many species of bird and fish may be observed here. Although it is worth touring, the site is slightly sterile, and moreover too popular.

Freeport

Pettengil Farm *(☎ 865-3170)* overlooks Harraseeket Estuary and features footpaths that meander about a salt-marsh.

 BICYCLING

The coast of Maine lends itself marvellously to bicycle touring. Route 1 leads to all the magnificent bays and villages that dot the coast. Moreover, as this region consists of a vast coastal plain, there are no endless ascents to negotiate. There is but one dark spot on the cycling horizon: traffic tends to very heavy during peak periods.

If you are unable, or disinclined, to bring your bicycle, it is simple to rent one. Here are some addresses:

Ogunquit

Classic Bikes
☎ 646-7909

Wheels and Waves
☎ 646-5774

The Kennebunks

Cape-Able Bike Shop
☎ 967-5181

Portland

Portland Recreation
☎ 874-8793

Forest City Mountain Bike Tours
☎ 780-8155

BOATING

How about a day of sailing, of being carried by the wind and the swells? Well, this daydream could become reality, even if you have no boat of your own. Many outfitters organise cruises on different types of craft, from antique turn-of-the-century sailboats and tall ships, to five-star cruise ships. Prices vary according to the type of boat and the length of the trip.

Ogunquit

Fineskind
P.O. Box 1828
departure from Barnacle Billy's Dock, at Perkins Cove
☎ 646-5227

The Bunny Clark
P.O. Box 837
departure from Town Dock, at Perkins Cove
☎ 646-2214

The Kennebunks

(see "Deep-sea Fishing", below)

Elizabeth 2
☎ 967-5595
(May to October)
Guided tours of 1 1/2 hours on the Kennebunk River and along the bay to Cape Porpoise.

Portland

Many companies organise cruises through the islands of Casco Bay. The islands number between 136 and 222 (there is no agreement on the exact number), and each has a unique mix of architectural attractions and little fishing villages.

Casco Bay Lines
Casco Bay Ferry Terminal
56 Commercial Street
☎ 774-7871

Eagle Tours
Long Wharf
☎ 774-6498 or 799-2872

Bay View Cruises
Fisherman's Wharf
☎ 761-0497

Freeport

Avatrice
Freeport Sailing Adventures
P.O. Box 303
☎ 854-6112
departure from Freeport
Town Wharf
(June to mid-October)

Atlantic Seal
25 Main Street,
P.O. Box 146
South Freeport ME 04078
☎ 865-6112
departure from Town Wharf
(May to October)

 DEEP-SEA FISHING

The fog slowly lifts over the bay. You hear the heavy footsteps on the dock. One by one, boat engines start their rumbling, rippling the mirror surface of the water. You approach a little, and see hard-featured lobster fishermen, their faces etched by salt-air, preparing for their day at sea.

Would you like to give lobster fishing a try, just for one day? Many fishermen take passengers on excursions along the coast, during which they lift their traps. It is a wonderful experience, and definitely recommended. Try to choose a smaller boat, to better appreciate the whole operation.

You can also partake of traditional fishing on the open sea. Boats leave from the ports of York, Ogunquit and Kennebunk for the best fishing spots. Among other species, you may land mackerel, shark, and pollack. Be suspicious of fish stories, though: after all, these are fishermen...

Kittery

Content
8 Forest Avenue
Eliot
☎ 439-5233
departure from Seaview Lobster
(June to the end of September)

The Yorks

F.V. Blackback
Seabury Charters Inc.,
P.O. Box 218
York ME 03909
☎ 363-5675
departure from Town Dock
No. 2
(May to October)

Shearwater
P.O. Box 472
departure from Town Dock
no 2
☎ 363-5324

The Boat, lobster fishing
excursions
10 Organug Road
York Harbour ME 03909
departure from Town Dock
No. 2
(June to September)

Ogunquit and Wells

MS Lainey
Bluefishing Plus
P.O. Box 1211
☎ 646-5046
departure from Perkins
Cove
(May 15th to October 1st)

Ugly Anne
P.O. Box 863
☎ 646-7202
departure from
Perkins Cove
(May to October)

The Kennebunks

Deep Water
Cape Arundel Cruises
P.O. Box 2775
departure from the Arundel
Boatyard-by-the-Bridge
(May to September)

Nereus
4 Western Avenue
☎ 967-5507
departure from the dock at
the same address
(May to October)

Portland

Devil's Den
P.O. Box 272
Scarborough
ME 04070-0272
☎ 761-44766
departure from DiMillo's Marina
(April and May; every day)

SEA KAYAKING

A sea kayaking adventure, which permits relatively unobtrusive up-close observation of animals, is truly unforgettable. The difference between river kayaking and sea kayaking is fundamental. The former involves a jittery, unstable little boat, ideal for running river rapids. The latter offers much more stability and comfort. Designed to master the waves and swells of the open sea, this small marine craft permits great manoeuvrability, and is as suited to the exploration of little bays as to excursions on the open sea.

An introductory course is strongly recommended before you plunge into the waves. The L.L. Bean store in Freeport organizes two events of particular interest to sea kayakers. The **L.L. Bean Sea Kayaking Symposium**, at the beginning of July, and the **L.L. Bean Coastal Kayaking Workshop**, at the beginning of August, offer introductory- to expert-level workshops. Most outfitters that organize sea kayaking excursions also provide introductory courses. For experienced kayakers, these same companies organize outings of many days' duration, guiding you through the islands that dot the coast of Maine.

Kennebunkport

Kayak Adventures
P.O. Box 943
ME 04046
☎ 967-5243

Portland

Maine Island Kayak Co.
70 Luther Street
Peak Island
☎ 766-2373,
or 1-800-769-2373

Maine Waters
76 Emery Street
ME 04102
☎ 871-0119

Nurumbega Outfitters
58 Fore Street
☎ 773-0910

 WHALE-WATCHING

As in most regions of northeastern North America, springtime sees the arrival in southern Maine of pods of whales. A whole gamut of cetaceans (common whale, blue whale, and many other species) can be observed, swimming side by side. One of the most popular spots for whale-watching is **Jeffrie's Ledge**, situated approximately 30 kilometres from Kennebunkport. It goes without saying that the Kennebunks count a multitude of boats that leave port every morning on whale-watching expeditions.

If you suffer from seasickness, be sure to board a larger boat, or go out on a morning when the sea is very calm. A whale-watching excursion makes for a wonderful time, and is sure to be successful (you will spot many whales).

The Kennebunks

Nautilus Whale Watch
P.O. Box 2775
departure   from
Boatyard-by-the-Bridge
☎ 967-0707
(May to October)

The Lion
departure from Nonantum
Hotel Marina
☎ 967-2921

Indian Whale Watch
departure   from   Arundel
Wharf Restaurant
☎ 967-5912
(July to October)

 SCUBA DIVING

The underwater exploration of Maine's coast constitutes an extraordinary experience. A few hours in the silence of the deep will calm even the rawest nerves, and the little bays along the coast harbour well-springs of fabulous treasures.

York

York Beach Scuba
Railroad Avenue
☎ 363-3330

 HIKING

No imposing mountains rose up along the southern coast of Maine, nor are there any long forest trails. However, seascape admirers will be delighted by the many little excursions that are possible. Moreover, various nature reserves, for example those bordering estuaries, are laid out with footpaths, perfect for easy strolls and outings with children.

York

Mount Agamenticus *(free; every day, from sunrise to sunset; access by Mountain Road, via Route 1, ☎ 363-1040)*, with its modest elevation of 200 metres, constitutes the highest summit between York and Florida. A little trail leads to the top of the mountain and offers breathtaking views of the Presidential Range and the Atlantic Ocean.

Wells

Wells National Estuarine Research Reserve at Laudholm Farm (see p 70).

Rachel Carson National Wildlife Refuge (see p 70).

Ogunquit

The **Marginal Way** follows the beach, a little over one kilometre, from Ogunquit's town centre to the pier at Perkins Cove. The product of a donation made in the 1920s by Josiah Chase, it offers visitors an exquisite encounter with the sea.

The Kennebunks

A few hundred metres east of Kennebunkport, the peninsula of **Vaughn's Island Preserve** (accessible on foot three hours prior to or after high tide) permits an excursion through a stand of tall trees.

Scarborough Marsh Nature Centre *(mid-June to September, 9:30am to 5:30pm; Pine Point Road, ☎ 883-5100)* constitutes the largest salt-marsh in Maine. Canoeing is possible, as are walking tours along footpaths.

Prouts Neck

Prouts Neck Cliff Path and Wildlife Sanctuary, between the cliffs and the sea, allows you to retrace the footsteps of painter Winslow Homer. The trail starts just past the Black Point Inn and hugs the coast, passing Eastern Point before returning to the inn. You can visit the **studio** *(July and August, 10am to 4pm; there is a sign marked, "studio", on a building adjacent to a private home)* where Homer created his universe of movements and war between man and the sea.

Portland

Many trails are maintained at **Gilsland Farm Sanctuary** *(free; every day, from sunrise to sunset; 118 Route 1, Falmouth Foreside, ☎ 781-2330)*.

Dating from 1814, **Fort Allan Park**, quietly defies the wind from atop a cliff. Another option for a stroll is the **Eastern Promenade**, designed by Frederick Law Olmsted, the same architect who graced Boston with its Emerald Necklace, New York with its celebrated Central Park, and Montreal with Parc du Mont-Royal. This walk is an excellent way to discover the architectural richness of Portland, as is the **Western Promenade**, which gives onto the Fore River.

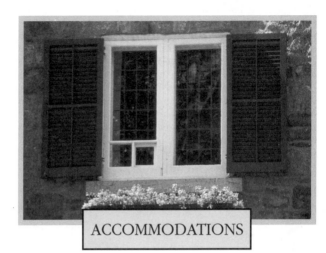

ACCOMMODATIONS

What would you say to a romantic stay in a Victorian B&B? You'll awaken slowly to the aroma of coffee and breakfast being prepared—and then decide to stay in bed anyway. Who cares what time it is? You're on vacation. Or perhaps you'd prefer a week (or two) at the seaside with the whole family. There, you could write an epic tale about valorous knights fighting fiercely for their lady amidst the area's numerous sandcastles. Anything is possible...

There is something for everyone on the coast of Maine, whether you're travelling by bus or by limousine. There are more or less four kinds of accommodations: campgrounds, motels, B&Bs and luxury hotels. The campgrounds and motels are located mainly along Route 1. Unfortunately, we can only bemoan the poor quality of these places, most of which are outdated and depressing. Their main attraction, obviously, is their price. A decent hotel room in the centre of town costs between $75 and $100, while you'll only have to pay about $50 for a room in a motel and $15 for a campsite. These places are also easy to find. As they are all pretty similar, we have only listed those that rate above average on the comfort and quality scale.

The next category of accommodations offers decidedly better value for money. There are scores of B&Bs along the coast of

Maine. Many are old houses run by the owners, and all have a distinctive charm and character about them. The hosts are gracious, the breakfasts delicious and the rooms very comfortable.

Finally, the luxury hotels all follow the same format, aside from a few minor differences. Most have a restaurant and a heated pool, and offer a wide range of activities. It goes without saying that the level of comfort is high and the service formal. On the down side, the prices tend to be elevated—often shamelessly.

Finally, don't forget that there is a 6% sales tax on all goods and services in the region.

 # KITTERY

Beautifully located on Kittery Point, the **Whaleback Inn** *($55-$65 bkfst incl.; P.O. Box 162, Pepperrell Road, ME 03905, ☎ 439-9570)* is sure to appeal to those who love peace and quiet. Each room is decorated in a different style or according to a different theme: Queen Anne, native American and toys. Guests also enjoy a view of Kittery Harbor and Portsmouth. The simple continental breakfast, served on the second floor, helps you start off the day on the right foot.

The **Gundalow Inn** *($80-$105; pb, ⊛; 6 Water Street, ME 03904, ☎ 439-4040)* is a magnificent Victorian house that has been converted into a B&B. It is easy to fall under the charm of one of the six rooms and the view of the Piscataqua River. The high level of comfort, fantastic service and top-notch breakfasts make this an address to remember in Kittery.

Enchanted Nights *($47-$135; Highway 103, 29 Wentworth Street, ME 03904-1720, ☎ 439-1489)*, run by a friendly couple from California, is another tastefully renovated Victorian. The unpretentious service always strikes the right note.

YORK HARBOR

Tea is served each afternoon at **Canterbury House** *($65-$110 bkfst incl.; pb; Highway 1A, P.O. Box 881, ME 03911, ☎ 363-3505)*. Imagine a warm summer day when the cool ocean air barely manages to dry the droplets of sweat forming on your neck as you sit in the shade on the balcony, watching the boats coming and going in York Harbor. This is what awaits you at this friendly little B&B. After a good night's sleep, you have the choice between a full or continental breakfast.

Patiently waiting atop its modest hill, the **Bell Buoy** *($70-$85; P.O. Box 445, 570 York Street, Highway 1A, ME 03911-0445, ☎ 363-7264)* offers simple accommodations. The owner's friendly, courteous service is perfectly suited to the turn-of-the-century Victorian house. You'll particularly appreciate the balcony overlooking the village of York and the relaxed atmosphere that prevails in this wooded setting. The rooms, of average dimensions, are economically priced.

The warm, enthusiastic welcome you'll receive at the **Inn at Harmon Park** *($69-$99 bkfst incl.; pb, ≡, ◎; 415 York Street, P.O. Box 495, ME 03911, ☎ 363-2031, ≈ 351-2948)* is one of the customs of the house. The owners who converted this late-19th-century Victorian have 10 years' experience as hosts, and it shows. After waking up slowly, you'll walk down to the terrace, where a good continental breakfast awaits. What more could you ask for?

The **Rivermer** *($75-$100; pb; 45 Varrell Lane, P.O. Box 141, ME 03911, ☎ 393-5470, ≈ 363-3268)* is an excellent option in this region. Its two rooms are relatively large, and the service is fantastic. You'll particularly appreciate the view of the harbour and the magnificent front garden.

A few steps from the beach, **Edward's Harborside Inn** *($90-$210 bkfst incl.; pb, P.O. Box 866, Stage Neck Road, ME 03911, ☎ 363-3037)* is an attractively decorated Victorian house dating from the beginning of the century. It has 10 rooms, ranging from a double room to a very luxurious suite, and scores high points for its courteous service. The continental breakfast served in the solarium will ease you into the morning rhythm of this spruce little town.

Decidedly one of the loveliest places to stay in the region, the **York Harbor Inn** *($99-$195; pb, ℛ, tv; Highway 1A, P.O. Box 573, ME 03911, ☎ 1-800-343-3869 or 363-5119, ✒ 363-3545)* combines luxury and good taste. Boasting a nearly century-old tradition of excellence, this inn succeeds in enchanting visitors year after year. The antique furniture and tasteful decor are particularly noteworthy. Each of the 36 rooms has a distinctive charm that lends the York Harbor Inn a unique atmosphere.

The **Dockside Guest Quarters** *($105-$150; pb, ℛ; tv; Harris Island, P.O. Box 205, ME 03909, ☎ 363-2868)* is set back from York Harbor. This complex, made up of a main building and a number of apartments, is an outstanding choice for visitors seeking peace and quiet. Here, you'll find the comfort and privacy necessary for complete relaxation just a short distance from York Village, with its beach and other attractions. The main building, built in the middle of the century and recently renovated, has four rooms overlooking the harbour. The studios, for their part, can comfortably accommodate three or four people. An excellent choice in this area.

Located at the mouth of the York River, the **Stage Neck Inn** *($135-$205; pb, ℛ, tv; P.O. Box 70, ME 03911, ☎ 1-800-222-3238 or 363-3850)* is very posh and has all the facilities standard at luxury hotels. The rooms are nondescript but comfortable, while the service, albeit cold and impersonal, is worthy of a grand hotel.

 YORK BEACH

The **Lighthouse Inn and Carriage House** *($95-$150; pb, ℛ, tv; P.O. Box 249, Nubble Road, ME 03910, ☎ 1-800-243-6072 or 363-6072)* offers good value for money and an attractive location. It's a big hotel and small inn combined. An excellent option for families.

Though it looks like some kind of monster defying the sea, the **Anchorage Inn** *($107-$265; pb, ℛ, tv; P.O. Box 265, Long Beach Avenue, ME 03910, ☎ 363-5112)* offers good value for money. The rooms look the same within each price range, but are all clean and comfortable. A very good choice for travellers looking for an affordable, well-located hotel where children are welcome.

Although its rooms are a little expensive, the **Union Bluff Hotel** *($118; pb, ℛ; Beach Street, P.O. Box 1860, ME 03910, ☎ 363-1333 or 1-800-833-0721)* wins the prize for distinctiveness. A white building several stories high, it looks like an old hotel in a 1950s movie. The modest but comfortable rooms offer an attractive view of the sea.

 ## OGUNQUIT

Located in the heart of the action in Ogunquit, the **Old Village Inn** *($65-85; pb, tv; 30 Maine Street, ME 03907, ☎ 646-7088)* offers excellent value for money. The decor is appropriate and simple, though the rooms are on the small side. The courteous, friendly service scores top marks.

The **Aspiniquid** *($110-$125; tv, pb; Beach Street, P.O. Box 2408, ME 03907, ☎ 646-7072, ⇐ 646-1187)* offers several interesting options, so don't be put off by its appearance. It rents out studios, apartments and rooms at reasonable rates, just minutes from the beach. The service is reserved, but the rooms are comfortable.

The eclectic ambiance of the **Yellow Monkey** *($65-$95 bkfst incl.; pb; 168 Maine Street, P.O. Box 478, ME 03907, ☎ 646-9056)* is sure to appeal to jovial types. The modest but comfortable rooms are good value, and the owner's cheerful hospitality always makes staying here a pleasure.

Upon entering the **Nellie Littlefield House** *($140-$185; pb, tv; 9 Shore Road, ME 03907, ☎ 646-1692)*, you'll feel as if you've stepped back in time. With its unpretentious service, top-quality, comfortable rooms and distinctive look, this place has a personality all its own.

The **Seacastle Resort** *($115-$190; pb, tv; 42 Shore Road, P.O. Box 816, ME 03907, ☎ 646-6055)* offers excellent value for your money. Located in the heart of Ogunquit, a few minutes from Perkins Cove, this place is perfect for families and travellers looking for affordably priced rooms.

The big **Colonial** *($73-$95; pb, tv; ☎ 646-5191 or 1-800-233-5191)* hotel complex is a mid-range option whose prices are moderate compared to the consistently higher rates of other local establishments. The rooms are standard but comfortable. Small, fully equipped apartments and studios are also available. Good value.

 KENNEBUNK

The **Kennebunk Inn** *($85-140; pb; 45 Main Street, Route 1, ME 04043, ☎ 985-3351 or 1-800-743-1799)* was once a doctor's office. The hushed atmosphere, antique furniture and sophisticated decor pay eloquent homage to the building's past. The rooms are comfortable but small. It is pleasant to top off the day here with a good scotch "from the old country".

 KENNEBUNKPORT

Located in the heart of Kennebunkport, the **English Meadows Inn** *($88-$135 bkfst incl.; pb, K; 141 Port Road, ME 04043, ☎ 967-5766 or 1-800-272-0698)* is a Victorian farmstead that has been converted into a B&B. The inn's character is well defined by its decor, featuring antiques laid out in the purest New England tradition. The spacious rooms, each with its own distinctive charm, are divided among two houses. Those in the main house are prettier and more luxurious, while the little studios in the other house are better suited to families, as they are equipped with a kitchenette.

The **Green Heron Inn** *($85-$135; 126 Ocean Avenue; P.O. Box 2578, ME 04046, ☎ 967-3315)*, facing the Kennebunkport harbour, offers good value. This place's appeal lies in its friendly, informal service and simple but comfortable rooms.

The **King's Port Inn** *($89-$175 bkfst incl.; pb; P.O. Box 1172, ME 04046, ☎ 1-800-286-5767, ≈ 967-4810)* offers a decent level of comfort and an advantageous location, just a few steps from Dock's Square. The rooms, though hardly dazzling, are decent. A good choice for visitors looking for affordable, well-located accommodations.

A Federal-style house dating from 1813, the **Captain Fairfield Inn** *($85-$135; pb; at the corner of Pleasant and Green Streets, P.O. Box 1308, ☎ 967-4454)* stands out for the quality of its service. Its comfortable rooms are attractively decorated with antiques and various objects harking back to the age of the great navigators. Inquire about seasonal discounts.

In addition to being beautiful, the **Maine Stay** *($125-$185; pb, tv; P.O. Box 500A, 24 Maine Street, ME 04046, ☎ 967-2117 or 1-800-950-2117, ⌐ 967-8757)* offers outstanding hospitality. This B&B, set up inside a house dating from 1860, is sure to charm even the most sceptical visitors.

The **Kennebunkport Inn** *($89-$219; pb, ℜ, tv; P.O. Box 111, Dock Square, ME 04046, ☎ 967-2621 or 1-800-248-2621)* looks like an English sitting room inside, but the rest of the place doesn't really measure up to expectation. The service is friendly and courteous, but the rooms are disappointing, considering how much they cost. They are nonetheless very comfortable, and being so close to Dock Square and all the action in the centre of town is a major plus.

At the **Captain Lord Mansion** *($150-$220; pb, tv; P.O. Box 800, ME 04046-0800, ☎ 967-3141, ⌐ 967-3172)*, another captain's house that has been converted into an inn, each room is lovelier than the last. The classical-style decor is sure to impress many visitors. One drawback, however, is the size of the rooms, which are very comfortable but relatively small.

A member of the prestigious Relais et Châteaux association, the **White Barn Inn** *($140-$320 bkfst incl.; pb, ℜ, tv; Beach Street, P.O. Box 560 C, ME 04046, ☎ 967-2321, ⌐ 967-1100)* is one of the most luxurious establishments in the region. The comfortable rooms, antique decor and attentive service have earned it international renown.

Don't expect to find anything out of the ordinary at the **Seaside Motor Inn** *($148-$168 bkfst incl.; pb, tv, Gooch's Beach, P.O. Box 631, ME 04046-0631, ☎ 967-4461)*. The rooms are modest and look outdated, but are nonetheless comfortable. Try to get one with a view of the ocean, the only real attraction this place has to offer.

KENNEBUNK BEACH

The **Sundial Inn** *($106, $156 bkfst incl.; tv; 48 Beach Street Avenue, P.O. Box 1147, ME 04043, ☎ 967-3850, ⚟ 967-4719)* will reassure visitors looking for a good, affordable place to stay. You'll enjoy relaxing on the balcony and watching the waves roll in. The rooms, generally on the small side, are very comfortable. Another plus is the living room, whose fireplace is particularly appealing on fall evenings.

You'll be welcomed with a smile at the **Ocean View** *($150-$195 bkfst incl.; pb; 72 Beach Avenue, ME 04043, ☎ and ⚟ 967-2750)*, a little farther along on Beach Avenue. Carole and Micheline make sure that your breakfast is a satisfying one, while Bob, with his wealth of information on what to see and do in the region, can help you find the perfect way to spend some lovely days in Maine. The rooms in the main house are full of charm and character, while the suites in the second building, the Ocean View Too, are more spacious and modern. Whichever room you choose, your stay here is sure to be memorable.

 CAPE PORPOISE

Sometimes, when researching a guide like this one, the author will unexpectedly come upon something truly special while rounding a bend in a country road or entering the curve of a bay. The **Inn at Harbour Head** *($170-$250 bkfst incl.; pb; 41 Pier Road, ME 04046-6919, ☎ 967-5564, ⚟ 967-1294)* was one of the most charming places we found while scouring the southern coast of Maine. The warm hospitality, attentive service, excellent breakfasts and undeniable comfort of the rooms guarantee a memorable stay. Factor in the peace and quiet of the village of Cape Porpoise, and you're in paradise.

 SACO

Built in 1827 in the neoclassical tradition, the **Crown 'n' Anchor Inn** *($65-$85 bkfst incl.; pb; P.O. Box 228, ME 04072-0228, ☎ 282-3829)* has been beautifully restored. Its six rooms all offer excellent value for the money. Considerable work went into decorating this extraordinary place. Take a few minutes to ask your host to tell you the tale of how he came to own the place.

 ## OLD ORCHARD

The Old Orchard area is abounding in hotels and motels of all different sorts. Unfortunately, as the years have gone by, many of these places have not made a sufficient effort to maintain a satisfactory level of quality. When checking in (especially if you are arriving without a reservation), you are strongly advised to visit the room beforehand. The railroad tracks that run through the village are another factor to keep in mind when choosing a place to stay; the nights can be long when you are constantly being disturbed.

As many travellers will want to camp out, we have listed a few decent campgrounds below. Camping is very popular in this region, so reservations are strongly recommended.

Bailey's Camping Resort: Highway 9 W. Scarborough, ☎ 883-6043.

Powder Horn Family Campground: Cascade Road, ☎ 934-4733 or 800-934-7038.

Old Orchard Beach Campground: Highway 5, Ocean Park Road, ME 04064, ☎ 934-4477.

Wagon Wheel Campground & Cabins: 3 Old Orchard Road, ME 04064, ☎ 934-2160.

The **Point of View Inn** *($40-$65 bkfst incl.; 3 Camp Comfort Avenue, ME 04064)*, located a few steps from the beach, has a simple, tasteful decor and an inviting atmosphere. The rooms are relatively standard but comfortable.

In contrast to the dubious-looking motels, there are a few places in the area that offer both comfort and charm. The **Carriage House** *($50-$110 bkfst incl.; pb; 24 Portland Avenue, ME 04064, ☎ 934-2141)* is a Victorian house with eight attractively furnished guest rooms. A five-room apartment is also available (the rate varies according to the number of occupants). The friendly, courteous service and tasty breakfasts guarantee a pleasant stay.

The **Atlantic Birches Inn** *($59-$120 bkfst incl.; pb; 20 Portland Avenue, ME 04064, ☎ 934-5295)*, another converted Victorian house, has six comfortable, well-decorated guest rooms. Come morning, you can savour a good cup of coffee in the shade of the birches before setting out to conquer the surf and sand here in Old Orchard Beach, a true swimming Mecca.

The **Beachfront Condotel** *($80-$175; pb, ⊛, K, tv; 1 Walnut Street, ME 04064; ☎ 934-7434)*, located right on the beach, has suites, studios and apartments. All the units are spacious and extremely comfortable. They are also equipped with a kitchenette, making this a perfect choice for families.

Well located just a few minutes' walk from the beach and the pier, the **Americana Motel** *($85-$125; pb, tv; at the corner of First and Heath Streets, ME 04046, ☎ 934-2292 or 1-800-656-9662)* has a homogeneous series of clean, well-kept rooms. Children are more than welcome; those under 16 stay for free. A good, affordable choice.

The **Grand View** *($65-195; pb, ⊛, tv; 189 East Grand Avenue, ME 04064, ☎ 934-4837 or 934-5600)*, also located along the beach, is a hodgepodge of condominiums, apartments and double rooms. All the units are comfortable and highly practical, with a nondescript modern decor.

A quintessential motel (that is, a huge building with homogeneous but comfortable rooms), the **Waves Motor Inn** *($90-$150; pb; 87 West Grand Avenue, ME 04064, ☎ 934-4949, ⇆ 934-5983)* has over 150 units. Despite its monstrously massive appearance, the complex offers good value. Try to get a room with a view of the sea, a treat for the eyes.

 ## PROUTS NECK

The **Black Point Inn** *($260-$300; pb, tv, ℜ; 510 Black Point Road, ME 04074, ☎ 883-4126, ⇆ 883-9976)* has been an integral part of the Prouts Neck landscape since 1878. A luxury hotel, it offers all the facilities typically found in this type of establishment. Travellers will particularly appreciate the panoramic view of the Atlantic and the outstanding comfort of the 80 rooms and six suites. The hotel also offers numerous activities (golf, beach, two swimming pools, two whirlpools and more). It is probably one of the most beautiful hotels in Maine, and visitors looking for comfort and pampering will be in heaven here.

 ## PORTLAND

As this Ulysses guide is devoted chiefly to the beaches of Maine, the section on Portland is rather succinct. We nevertheless thought it would be a good idea to include a few listings for hotels likely to appeal to our readers. Bear in mind, however, that there are scores of places to stay in Portland, no matter what your budget.

The **Hotel Everett** *($35-$49; 51A Oak Street, ☎ 773-7882)* and **Portland Hall** *($20, dormitory; 645 Congress Street, ☎ 874-3281)* both offer quality accommodations at very low rates. The latter belongs to the American Youth Hostel Association.

Recently renovated in order to restore its 1927 lustre, the **Eastland Plaza Hotel** *($80-$135 bkfst incl.; pb, ℜ; 157 High Street, ME 04101, ☎ 775-5411 or 1-800-777-5246)* really gives you your money's worth. It has 204 spacious, attractively decorated rooms. Try to get one with a view of the harbour.

The **Inn on Carleton Street** *($95-$135 bkfst incl.; pb; 46 Carleton Street, ME 04102, ☎ 775-1910)* stands out for its hospitality. Well located, this comfortable inn decorated with Victorian antiques is sure to satisfy even the most discerning travellers.

The **Pomegranate Inn** *($125-$165 bkfst incl.; pb, tv; 49 Neal Street, ☎ 772-1006 or 1-800-356-0408)* has eight rooms. The owners clearly have an eye for tasteful decoration. Each room has something special about it, be it the antique furniture, the wallpaper or the drapes: everything is outstanding. A wonderful place, but a bit expensive.

RESTAURANTS

In addition to beautiful natural landscapes, the coast of Maine is home to a whole gamut of restaurants that will satisfy even the pickiest gourmets. As well, from village to village, there is a little bit of everything for everybody. Naturally, seafood is most prominent in the culinary masterpieces of the coast. Lobster, clams, salmon, shrimp, and more will tempt your appetite. But seafood is not all. At the end of one country road is a wonderful Italian restaurant, and there is an excellent French restaurant in the heart of Ogunquit. Ultimately, you will be surprised by the epicurean pleasures Maine has in store.

Unfortunately, some areas display the relatively limited culinary landscape of endless fast-food stands, where hamburgers, pizza, and French fries are lunchtime fare. Be alert, moreover, for exorbitant prices at these places, which are mostly interested in your precious dollars. We have thought it ill-advised to list restaurants that proffer little more than frozen french fries. These same swarm around the beaches and are hard to miss.

Establishments are classified according to their geographic location. Each listing includes a description of the restaurant's cuisine and atmosphere, as well as a price quotation relative to the four pricing categories used in this guide. For dinner, main dishes at "budget" restaurants generally cost $8 or less (*$*); the ambience is informal and the service is satisfactory. Establishments in the moderate price range (*$$*) offer meals between $8 and $16; the atmosphere is casual but pleasant, the menu is more varied, and the service is usually less hasty. In the moderate-high category (*$$$*), the main course rises to more than $16; the cuisine varies from simple to elaborate, but the decor is always more sumptuous and the service more personalized. Establishments in the most expensive category (*$$$$*) have no main dish for less than $24, and gourmets will find themselves pleasantly rewarded; the cuisine is (as one would expect) a refined art, and the service is meticulous.

Some restaurants close for the winter season.

For breakfast and lunch, prices vary less from one restaurant to another. Even establishments in the moderate-high category generally offer light meals morning and noon for at most a few dollars more than budget restaurants. These more modest meals provide an opportunity to try some of the more stylish restaurants.

The prices mentioned in this guide apply, except where otherwise indicated, to a meal for one person, excluding tip and beverages.

$	less than 8 $US
$$	8 $ to 16 $US
$$$	16 $ to 24 $US
$$$$	more than 24 $US

 KITTERY

If you are looking for a happening place, or if you are having trouble waking up one morning, **Friendly Toast** *($-$$; 19 Bridge Street, ☎ 439-2882)* is just the spot. It features an eclectic menu, from magnificent pancakes to home-made fries, and everything is delicious and served with a smile. Particularly enjoyable is the decor, composed of knick-knacks culled from our collective consumerist past. Apparently kitsch is back in fashion. Friendly Toast is worth the trip.

For American-style seafood (fried, and served with French fries and coleslaw) **Bob's Clam Hut** *($-$$; Route 1, ☎ 439-4233)* is a required stop. Meals are taken quickly at picnic tables, in a simple atmosphere.

Savour mouth-watering boiled lobster in the enchanting, plush, relaxed surroundings of **Cap'n Simeon's Galley** *($-$$; Pepperell Cove, Kittery Point, ☎ 439-3655)*. From the dining room overlooking the dock of Kittery Point, you can watch fishermen returning to the village after a long day at sea. Highly recommended.

With a regional reputation for the quality of its seafood, **Warrens Lobster House** *($$; Route 1, ☎ 439-1630)* needs little introduction. Treat yourself to the Lobster Oscar: lobster meat sauteed in butter, sprinkled with Béarnaise sauce, and served with asparagus. It is a genuine delight!

A few minutes' walk from the sprawling shopping centres of Kittery, **Weathervane** *($$; Route 1, ☎ 439-0330)* offers a menu primarily composed of seafood and grill dishes. The decor is profoundly lacking in charm, as is characteristic of this type of chain restaurant. However, the food is good and replenishes after long hours of impassioned shopping.

 ## THE YORKS

For a quiet dinner that will not cost your vacation allowance, **Dockside Restaurant** *($-$$; closed Monday; Route 103, York Harbour, ☎ 363-2722)* is the place. The menu, which combines local specialties and catches of the day, offers an excellent price-quality ratio. Set back from the village, the restaurant has a peaceful, relaxed atmosphere.

Fazio's *($-$$; 38 Woodbridge Road, ☎ 363-7019)* serves a variety of Italian dishes in a rather ordinary decor. The price-quality ratio is excellent, though, and the service exemplary. This restaurant is a very good spot for family dining.

The Bluff *($-$$; Beach Street, ☎ 363-1333)* is a little restaurant with the look of a London pub. Savour simple, well-prepared cuisine, in a warm, relaxed atmosphere. The menu is composed of seafood and grill dishes, as well as a good selection of soups and salads, for those in the mood for a lighter meal after a long day in the sun.

Simple decor, an extraordinary view of the sea and an impressive seafood menu add up to **Fox Lobster House** *($$; Nubble Point Road, York Beach, ☎ 363-2643)*. The service is courteous and quick, and there is lobster prepared in a hundred and one ways.

The easy-going accents of Italian-America are audible as you enter **Mimmo's** *($$; Route 1A, York Beach, ☎ 363-3807)*. You would believe yourself transported to the filmic universe of Scorsese and Coppola, where everybody knows each other, loves each other, and yells at each other. Back in reality, Mimmo's offers a menu of pasta, seafood, and Italian specialties, such as chicken Rollatini (garnished with prosciutto, and served in a sauce of wine and mushrooms). A menu beyond compare and a pleasant family ambience merit this establishment a heartfelt, *"molto bene!"*.

Decorated like an old-fashioned barn, the **Lobster Barn** *($$; Route 1, York, ☎ 363-4721)* boasts a seafood menu to please the whole family. The efficient, congenial service has attracted crowds for several decades now.

Between the ocean and The Anchorage Inn (see p 84), **Sun-n-Surf** *($$-$$$; Long Beach Avenue, ☎ 363-2961)* proposes a menu combining seafood and grill selections. During warmer months, the restaurant opens its magnificent terrace looking out onto the sea, the perfect spot for a long, languorous summer supper.

The restaurant at **York Harbour Inn** *($$$; Route 1A, ☎ 363-5119)* is as lovely as the hotel (see p 84). In a warm, classic atmosphere, lit by a fireplace, it offers a menu of regional specialties.

Cape Neddick Inn *($$$; 1233 Route 1, ☎ 363-2899)* proposes refined and delectable French cuisine. Mouths water at the mere mention of its name, thanks to such delights as salmon filet in fine herbs and sirloin pepper steak. All are served courteously in an elegant and plush decor.

OGUNQUIT AND WELLS

Little **Einstein's Deli** *($; 2 Shore Road, Ogunquit, ☎ 646-5262)* will please travellers seeking economy and a flavoursome menu. Simple and unpretentious, this restaurant proves very charming.

Curiously, **Barnacle Billy's** *($-$$; Perkins Cove, ☎ 646-5575)* is a veritable institution in the region. Tourists clamour to sit at picnic tables and eat lobster from paper baskets. The atmosphere is unpretentious, but the very reasonable prices meet the mark.

Well-situated on the point at Perkins Cove, **Hurricane** *($-$$; Perkins Cove, ☎ 646-6348)* offers a good price-quality ratio. The expeditious service represents the only drawback of this nice little restaurant. It is good spot for breakfast, and the seafood salads are thoroughly succulent.

Valerie's *($$; Route 1, ☎ 646-2476)* has maintained its excellent local reputation for over 50 years. The exaggerated decor has nothing to do with the quality of the dining. The home-made Greek specialties are delightful.

With its English sitting room decor, **Old Village Inn** *($$; 30 Main Street, Ogunquit, ☎ 646-7088)* has a distinguished air without any concomitant price inflation. The friendly service is praiseworthy, but the main attraction is the creative menu, which includes pasta in almost every imaginable sauce.

98 Provence *($$-$$$; 98 Provence Street, Ogunquit, ☎ 646-9898)* figures as one of the best restaurants in the area. The owners, originally from Montreal, specialize in fine French cuisine, including such dishes as *escargots* in puff pastry, *panachés* of endives, salmon escalopes, and thick venison steaks garnished with Morello cherries. Could anyone ask for more? A little romance perhaps...

Many food critics have named it the best restaurant in Maine, and **Arrow's** *($$$; Berwick Road, ☎ 361-1100)* continues to impress more than a few clients. Every dish is based on regional specialties, except that the two chefs share a penchant for experimentation (contributing to your greater culinary pleasure). The lobster, unlike any you have tasted, is an experience in itself.

 THE KENNEBUNKS

A good spot for a family breakfast, **The Green Heron** *($; Ocean Avenue, Kennebunkport, ☎ 967-3315)* is highly recommended. The classics — bacon and eggs, pancakes, etc. — are served in an unpretentious atmosphere.

Situated on Dock Square (see p 54), **Alysson's** *($; 5 Dock Square, ☎ 967-4841)* proposes a simple family menu of well-prepared dishes. The informal and attentive service is appreciated by a regular clientele drawn by the famous lobster roll, reputed to be the best in town.

It is not easy to find, but **ImPASTAble Dream** *($-$$; 17 Main Street, Kennebunk, ☎ 985-6039)* is worth seeking out. Treat yourself to Italian specialties and take the time to savour them, all the while knowing that the bill will be just as agreeable an experience. Surely, this is one of the nicest surprises in the region.

Arundel Wharf Restaurant *($$; 43 Ocean Avenue, Kennebunkport, ☎ 967-3444)* presents a vast array of seafood at affordable prices. Moreover, the location of the restaurant beside the quay permits you to enjoy a good meal as you watch boats returning to port, lit by the pale rays of the setting sun.

In the heart of Kennebunk, **Kennebunk Inn** *($$-$$$; 45 Main Street, Kennebunk, ☎ 985-3351)* has been recognized time and time again for the quality dining experience it provides. In this warm, traditional atmosphere is served a multitude of dishes each one as sumptuous as the next. Whether it is Greek-style chicken or seafood fettucini, the fare is delightful.

Seascape *($$$; Pier Road, Cape Porpoise, ☎ 967-8500)*, perched on the quay at Cape Porpoise, has forged an excellent reputation thanks to the quality of its dishes and the view that can be enjoyed from its dining-room. This establishment also won the "Wine Spectator's Award" in 1994 for its impressive wine cellar. Treat yourself to the lobster, among the best in the area.

White Barn Inn *($$$; Beach Street, Kennebunkport, ☎ 967-2321)* has won all of the most prestigious awards. The menu is composed of refined dishes, all served in a posh atmosphere. Amateurs might want to bone up on their table etiquette, including the use of the appropriate fork.

 # OLD ORCHARD BEACH

In Old Orchard, more that in other towns along the coast, there is an abundance of fast-food restaurants. Tucked between souvenir shops, hamburger, pizza, and hot-dog stands line the beach and the Pier (see p 58).

A good spot in terms of price-quality ratio, **Danton's Family Restaurant** *($; Old Orchard Street, ☎ 934-7701)* has been serving home-style meals since 1946. The desserts are fabulous.

Bayley's Lobster Pound *($-$$; East Grand Avenue, Scarborough, ☎ 883-4571)* is the place for inexpensive seafood. Crab, lobster, oysters and shrimp are the highlights at this simple, agreeable restaurant.

Cornforth House *($-$$; 893 Route 1, Saco, ☎ 284-2006)* occupies a large red house in Saco. Separate little dining-rooms give this establishment an intimate feeling. The restaurant offers excellent cuisine based on house seafood specialties. Unequivocally, highly recommended.

For its part, **Village Inn** *($-$$; 213 Saco Avenue, Old Orchard Beach, ☎ 934-7370)* posts a varied menu combining seafood and grill dishes. The seafood "combo" is delicious, not to mention enormous.

Much acclaimed, **Joseph By The Sea** *($$-$$$; 57 West Grand Avenue, Old Orchard Beach, ☎ 934-5044)* tantalizes local and long-travelled taste buds alike. Romantic decor distinguishes this establishment, but the main attraction is the creative menu. There is dining on the terrace in warmer months.

PROUTS NECK

Renown for its long tradition of excellence as an inn, the **Black Point Inn** *($$-$$$; 510 Black Point Road, ☎ 883-4126)* is equally recommended for its restaurant. The exquisite cuisine and luxurious atmosphere gratify on every occasion.

 PORTLAND

Beer lovers will appreciate **Gritty's Pub** *($-$$; 396 Fore Street, ☎ 772-2739)*. This little establishment is ideal for a quick bite and a glass of good home-made beer. A relaxed ambience and friendly service also figure well.

A classic in the region, **Old Port Tavern** *($-$$; 11 Moulton Street, ☎ 774-0444)* welcomes a mixed and lively clientele. Moreover, the cuisine is beyond compare and the service is flawless.

Despite the service, which is a little nonchalant, **Walter's Café** *($-$$; 15 Exchange Street, ☎ 871-9258)* redeems itself admirably thanks to the quality of its cuisine. A meal here is made even more enjoyable by wonderful jazz music. What could be better than an espresso savoured at the end of a meal to the tune of *So What* by Miles Davis?

T.G.I. Friday's *($-$$; 311 Fore Street)* satisfies the truly ravenous. This bar for devoted sports fans, decorated with giant screens and posters of professional sports heroes, proposes a menu of grill dishes. The portions are immense, the beer flows freely, and service very buddy-buddy!

The menu of **Wharf Street Café** *($-$$; 38 Wharf Street, ☎ 773-6667)* is divided into two sections, small and large, which share quality as a common denominator. Dining is set in a warm, traditional environment. Recommended.

Katahdin *($-$$; 106 Hugh Street, ☎ 774-1740)* has established a reputation thanks to the unpretentious, family-style welcome it reserves for its clients. The menu, essentially composed of fish and grill items (the trout is delicious), satisfies those interested in a good price-quality ratio.

Street and Co. *($-$$; 33 Wharf Street, ☎ 775-0887)* varies its menu according to the catch of the day. Diners are thereby assured of quality meals at affordable prices. Friendly, elegant ambience contributes to the mood.

Perfetto *($$; 28 Exchange Street, ☎ 828-0001)* proposes a menu of pasta dishes prepared in purest Italian-American fashion. The service is meticulous, and the traditional atmosphere is charming.

Khalidi's *($$; 36 Market Street, ☎ 871-1881)* specializes in Maine staples, fish and seafood. The menu varies according to the catch of the day, assuring fresh and succulent dishes. Sauteed shrimp on a bed of spinach fettucini is just one of the many temptations. Sheer delight.

ENTERTAINMENT

I t would be a mistake to believe that your enjoyment of Maine is limited to daylight hours — the moon shines brightly too. Every little town has a pub that attracts a clientele of regulars and travellers around a draft, a scotch, a Bailey's, a rum and Coke... Going out is a must. Who knows what you might find as you explore these nocturnal hideaways?

 KITTERY

With its ultra-kitsch lounge atmosphere, **Friendly Toast** *(19 Bridge Street, ☎ 439-2882)* is a good spot to savour a warm Guinness. The service is friendly, and the clientele is relatively young and eclectic.

 YORK

For an evening at the cinema, **York Beach Cinema** *(6 Beach Street, ☎ 363-2074)* presents current Hollywood releases.

Adjacent to **Union Bluff Hotel** *(Beach Street, ☎ 363-1333)* is a pleasant little bar that serves a clientele of regulars and the occasional hotel patron. Although it is unexceptional, it has a pleasant ambience, and you can actually have a conversation without shouting.

 OGUNQUIT

Established in 1932, **Ogunquit Playhouse Theater** *(every day except Sunday, end of June to Labour Day;* ☎ *646-5511)* presents several plays and musical comedies each summer. This is one of the top-ranked summer theatres in the United States.

Little **Albert's Café** *(2 Shore Road, Ogunquit,* ☎ *646-5262)*, really has nothing extraordinary about it, but everybody gathers here at the end of the day. Consequently it has a friendly ambience. You can also get a bite to eat here.

Two recently renovated old cinemas present the most recent Californian "explosions": **Leavitt Fine Arts Theater** *(Route 1,* ☎ *646-3123)*, and **Ogunquit Square Theater** *(Shore Road,* ☎ *646-5151)*.

 KENNEBUNKPORT

Federal Jack's Brew Pub *(8 Western Avenue,* ☎ *967-4322)* welcomes crowds of celebrants from the whole region. This establishment brews its own beers and the red ale makes a visit well-worthwhile. There are a few pool tables and often live music is presented.

 OLD ORCHARD

The **Pier** is host to, without a doubt, the largest concentration of revellers in southern Maine. Come nightfall, all of Old Orchard gathers for a drink and a dance among friends. There is a country bar at the end of the pier, and a series of fast-food stands satisfy those midnight cravings.

 PORTLAND

Music

Music lovers in-the-know frequent City Hall Auditorium to be enraptured by beautiful classical symphonies. The **Portland Symphony Orchestra** *(October to April, Tuesday at 7:45, City Hall Auditorium, 339 Congress Street; in summer the orchestra tours from town to town; ☎ 773-8191)* presents classical music programs year-round.

Two other organisations present classical music concerts throughout the city and the state. The **Lark Society for Chamber Music/Portland String Quartet** *(☎ 761-1522)* specialises in chamber music, and the **Portland Concert Association** *(☎ 772-8630)* shows an affinity for jazz and classical music.

Theatre

Two troupes share the stage at the **Portland Performing Arts Center** *(25A Forest Street)*: **Portland Stage Company** *(☎ 774-0465)* and **Ram Island Dance Company** *(☎ 773-2562)*. The former stages diverse theatre pieces from September to April, while the latter presents dance performances every weekend, year-round.

Bars

A classic in the region, **Gritty McDuff's Brew Pub** *(396 Fore Street, ☎ 772-2739)* brews its own beer. A very good bitter and an excellent stout figure on the menu of this English-style pub. It draws a regular clientele that comes to celebrate among friends.

Guinness lovers meet at **Brian Borù** *(57 Center Street, ☎ 780-2787)* to sanctify the advertising slogan: "Guinness, not just for breakfast any more".

For alternative rock, with a bit of jazz and reggae, **Zoots** *(31 Forest Avenue,* ☎ *773-8187)* is the place. It has two bars and a dance floor where the young clientele lives it up. There is a cover charge on weekends and for concerts.

If you like unpretentious pubs where everybody knows each other, **Three Dollar Dewey's** *(241 Commercial Street,* ☎ *772-8187)* is just up your alley. In a warm, unaffected atmosphere you can choose from a vast selection of imported beers. The clientele is composed of regulars, some of whom apparently while away countless hours here.

SHOPPING

Southern Maine is a shop-a-holic's paradise. People come here by the busload to stock up at the factory outlets in Freeport and Kittery, where you can find just about everything—antiques, trendy underwear, haute couture, art galleries, bookstores, crafts, flower shops, tents, etc. In certain cases, shoppers enjoy major discounts on well-known brands, but it is a common misconception that everything is less expensive here. Each factory outlet carries a single brand of merchandise, more or less. There are big discounts on defective items (the defects in question are generally so minor as to be barely noticeable) and more moderate rebates on regular merchandise.

According to the merchants, the main reason they can offer these discounts is that the cost of renting space here is so much less than on Fifth Avenue in New York. They therefore pass on some of the savings to their customers. There's a trick, though: some companies have both a factory outlet and a regular store here, so you'll see some reduced items, and others at full price. Furthermore, some retailers, like Calvin Klein, don't have a factory outlet, but rather a company store, where certain articles are less expensive. Our advice: be vigilant. Also, try to anticipate the peak shopping periods; at Christmas, the place gets so crowded that it becomes absolutely unbearable.

FACTORY OUTLETS

 ## Kittery

Above, we used the term "shop-a-holic's paradise", and here's why: nearly 115 stores—Guess, Timberland Shoes, Converse, Boss, Liz Claiborne, Levi's, Anne Klein, Calvin Klein and many others—lining a stretch of road just two kilometres long. Because Kittery is less popular than Freeport (home of the L.L. Bean), and thus has to try harder to attract consumers, the local merchants tend to really slash prices. Furthermore, the retailers in this little town will tell anyone willing to listen that all the stores here are real factory outlets.

All these outlets are located on Highway 1, between Highway 236 to the west and Haley Highway to the east.

 ## Freeport

It all started here, with the founding of the outdoor clothing company **L.L. Bean**. In 1912, Leon Leonwood Bean invented a particularly well-designed pair of boots for hunting and fishing. He started out selling these rubber-soled leather boots by mail. Having noticed that many hunters stayed overnight in his town, he eventually decided to keep his store open around the clock, 365 days a year. The family-run business got lots of good press, and gradually expanded to its present size. Today, L.L. Bean is a veritable institution, a shrine around which a host of factory outlets and specialized shops prostrate themselves. L.L. Bean, of course, specializes in outdoor clothing and equipment. You'll find everything here, from gloves to canoes. It really is worth taking the time to explore this temple of consumerism. The place is so big and so full of frenzied shoppers that it's easy to get lost!

L.L. Bean's resounding success prompted other companies to set up shop in Freeport. There are now nearly 110 stores here to satisfy your wildest shopping desires—at discount prices to boot. Among these are the Gap, Calvin Klein, Polo Ralph Lauren, Crabtree & Evelyn, Levi's, Reebok, Rockport, etc. With such an impressive list of major brand names, it is no wonder that people flock here. Come summer, the shopping mania is infectious; you'd think you were at a carnival. We should add that there is plenty of space to park behind the stores. A word of advice: arrive early in the morning; shopping here during the day can be unbearable.

To get to Freeport, head east on the I-95. Take Exit 19 South, and follow Main Street to bargainland.

 ANTIQUES

Over the years, Maine has built itself a solid reputation among antique collectors. Visitors will thus find a large number of shops specializing in all that is old. It is often possible to unearth restored pieces of antique furniture that bear witness to the state's history. Below, we have listed a few places where you might discover a real treasure. Watch out for fake antiques (meaning new furniture made to look old); the difference has less to do with quality than price. What's more, real antiques have a genuine historical value.

 York

York Antiques Gallery
Highway 1
☎ 363-5002
Year round, every day 10am to 5pm

Cranberry Hill
Highway 1
☎ 363-5178
Year round, 9am to 5pm, closed Wednesday

 Ogunquit

R. Jorgensen
Highway 1
☎ 646-9444
Year round, 10am to 5pm, closed Wednesday

Kenneth & Ida Manko
Seabreeze Avenue
☎ 646-2565
May to October (by appointment during winter); every day 9am
to 5pm

 Wells

Wells Union Antiques Center
Highway 1
☎ 646-6612
Every day
About 15 antique dealers under one roof.

Douglas N. Harding
Highway 1
☎ 646-8785
Year round, 9am to 5pm, July and August 9am to 9pm

MacDougall-Gionet
Highway 1
☎ 646-3531
Year round, 9am to 5pm; closed Monday

 Kennebunk

Antiques on Nine
Highway 9
☎ 967-0626
Year round, Monday to Sunday 9am to 5pm

 BOOKSTORES

In addition to a few good places for rare books, there are many
stores where you can stock up on literature; after all, you have
to protect your brain from solar overload!

Wells

Douglas N. Harding
Highway 1
☎ 967-0626
Rare books specialist.

The Book Barn
Highway 1
☎ 646-4926

East Coast Books
Highway 1
☎ 646-3584

Austin's Antiquarian Bookstore
Highway 1
☎ 646-4883

 Kennebunkport

The Kennebunk Book Port
10 Dock Square
☎ 967-3815 or 800-382-2710
Set up inside a former rum distillery dating from 1775, this charming little store has a rich collection of books, including a vast selection of volumes on Maine and the sea.

 Freeport

DeLorme's Map Store
Highway 1
☎ 865-4126
DeLorme's is a veritable institution as far as road maps are concerned. It sells maps, atlases and numerous travel guides on U.S. destinations.

Portland

Books Etc.
38 Exchange Street

Raffle's Cafe Bookstore
55 Congress Street
A bookstore that serves light meals. What could be better than
an espresso and a good book?

 SOUVENIRS

 York

York Village Crafts
211 York Street
☎ 363-4830
Every day 9am to 5pm
Set up inside a church dating from 1834, this shop sells objets
d'art, antiques and local crafts. A good place to find gifts for
the folks back home.

 Kennebunkport

The Good Earth
Dock Square
☎ 967-4635
Closed from December 25 to May 15
Stoneware items that make good gifts. A little treasure trove.

 Portland

Abacus
44 Exchange Street
☎ 772-4880
A shop specializing in American crafts. Over 600 artisans
represented.

The Maine Potter's Market
376 Fore Street
☎ 774-1633
If you're looking for ceramics, this is the place to go. A vast selection of traditional and avant-garde pieces.

INDEX

■ ULYSSES TRAVEL GUIDES

☐ Affordable Bed & Breakfasts in
   Québec . . . . $12.95 CAN
   $9.95 US
☐ Beaches of Maine . . . . $12.95 CAN
   $9.95 US
☐ Canada's Maritime
   Provinces . . . . $24.95 CAN
   $14.95 US
☐ Chicago . . . . $19.95 CAN
   $14.95 US
☐ Cuba . . . . $24.95 CAN
   $16.95 US
☐ Dominican Republic . . . $24.95 CAN
   $17.95 US
☐ Ecuador Galapagos
   Islands . . . . $24.95 CAN
   $17.95 US
☐ El Salvador . . . . $22.95 CAN
   $14.95 US
☐ Guadeloupe . . . . $24.95 CAN
   $16.95 US
☐ Honduras . . . . $24.95 CAN
   $16.95 US
☐ Martinique . . . . $24.95 CAN
   $16.95 US
☐ Montréal . . . . $19.95 CAN
   $14.95 US
☐ Nicaragua . . . . $24.95 CAN
   $16.95 US
☐ Ontario . . . . $24.95 CAN
   $14.95 US
☐ Panamá . . . . $24.95 CAN
   $16.95 US
☐ Portugal . . . . $24.95 CAN
   $16.95 US

☐ Provence - Côte
   d'Azur . . . . $24.95 CAN
   $14.95US
☐ Québec . . . . $24.95 CAN
   $14.95 US
☐ Toronto . . . . $18.95 CAN
   $13.95 US
☐ Vancouver . . . . $14.95 CAN
   $10.95 US
☐ Western Canada . . . . . $24.95 CAN
   $16.95 US

■ ULYSSES GREEN ESCAPES

☐ Cycling in France . . . . $22.95 CAN
   $16.95 US
☐ Hiking in the Northeastern
   United States . . . . $19.95 CAN
   $13.95 US
☐ Hiking in Québec . . . . . $19.95 CAN
   $13.95 US

■ ULYSSES DUE SOUTH

☐ Acapulco . . . . $14.95 CAN
   $9.95 US
☐ Cartagena (Colombia) . $9.95 CAN
   $5.95 US
☐ Cancun Cozumel . . . . . $17.95 CAN
   $12.95 US
☐ Puerto Vallarta . . . . . . $14.95 CAN
   $9.95 US
☐ St. Martin and St. Barts $16.95 CAN
   $12.95 US

■ ULYSSES TRAVEL JOURNAL

☐ Ulysses Travel Journal . $9.95 CAN
   $7.95 US

QUANTITY	TITLES	PRICE	TOTAL

	Sub-total	
NAME:_____	Postage & Handling	$8.00*
ADDRESS:_____	Sub-total	
_____	G.S.T.in Canada 7%	
_____	TOTAL	

Payment: ☐ Money Order ☐ Visa ☐ MasterCard
Card Number:_____Exp.:_____
Signature:_____

ULYSSES TRAVEL PUBLICATIONS
4176 Saint-Denis, Montréal, Québec, H2W 2M5
(514) 843-9447 fax (514) 843-9448
*$15 for overseas orders